Bonsai
basics

A Pyramid Gardening Paperback

Bonsai
basics

Colin Lewis

hamlyn

An Hachette UK Company
www.hachette.co.uk

A Pyramid Paperback

First published in Great Britain in 1997
by Hamlyn, an imprint of
Octopus Publishing Group Ltd,
Carmelite House
50 Victoria Embankment
London EC4Y 0DZ
www.octopusbooks.co.uk
www.octopusbooksusa.com

Revised edition published 2005
This edition published in 2008

Copyright © Octopus Publishing Group Ltd
2005, 2008

Distributed in the US by
Hachette Book Group,
1290 Avenue of the Americas
4th and 5th Floors
New York, NY 10104

Distributed in Canada by
Canadian Manda Group
664 Annette Street
Toronto, Ontario, Canada M6S 2C8

This material was previously published as
Bonsai: A Hamlyn Care Manual

Colin Lewis asserts the moral right to be
identified as the author of this work.

ISBN 978-0-600-61910-9

A CIP catalogue record for this book is available
from the British Library

Printed and bound in China

25 24 23

Executive Editor Sarah Ford
Editor Alice Tyler
Executive Art Editor Karen Sawyer
Designer 'ome design
Production Controller Nosheen Shan

Contents

Introduction

For most people, their first encounter with bonsai is probably in a department store or garden nursery during the pre-Christmas shopping panic. Each year, many thousands of little trees are imported from China, Japan and other Far-Eastern countries to satisfy the gift market. Sadly, most of these will die – either through neglect or, ironically, more often through excessive care by their enthusiastic new owners. This fact is all the more sad because the initial disappointment often deters the novice from progressing further, and an opportunity to develop a thoroughly rewarding and satisfying new hobby is lost.

In fact, keeping a bonsai alive and healthy is not significantly more difficult than caring for any other potted plant, provided you understand the difference between an ordinary plant pot and a shallow bonsai container, and you are aware of the requirements of the particular species in question. The watering, feeding and pruning of bonsai are straightforward gardening techniques which can be learnt easily and quickly, even by someone with no prior experience of dealing with plants.

The practical skills required to maintain and develop the shape of a bonsai are also very easy to acquire. Pruning roots and branches, pinching out growing shoots and shaping branches with wire are all simple techniques that are identical to those employed by the most revered Japanese masters. Once learnt, they are never forgotten and will enable you to progress your bonsai hobby as far as you want.

Of course, you may well be content with just one or two bonsai to decorate your home or garden. But the chances are that you will be so fascinated by the challenge and reward of cultivating miniaturized trees that you will, in time, become totally hooked. Your collection will grow and your thirst for more detailed and advanced knowledge will grow with it. You may seek the advice of more experienced bonsaiists you meet at your local nursery, or you may subscribe to some of the specialist magazines that are now available. However, by far the best way to progress is to join a local bonsai club or study group.

Bonsai clubs provide their members with visiting teachers, lecturers, practical workshops, libraries and many other learning aids. But the most valuable asset of all is the contact you will have with other like-minded bonsai enthusiasts of all levels of ability and experience. They will always be ready to offer advice and guidance and, before you know it, you too will be advising new members who come to their first meeting bursting with questions.

One final point. It is always worth remembering that even the top Japanese and Chinese bonsai masters were once beginners themselves, ignorant of the techniques that this art form requires. Many of them had to learn the hard way – through trial and error, and by experiment. Their wisdom has been passed on to others, in the East and the West, and is now available to you through the pages of this book, enabling you to gain the knowledge you will need quickly and easily.

Colin Lewis

So what is a bonsai?

To some people, a bonsai is a cruelly stunted tree, confined in a too-small pot. To others, it is a work of art, resulting from many years of patient care and attention. To the vast majority, it is a fascinating miniature representation of a natural tree form, providing its owner with year-round interest and a highly satisfying pastime.

So what is a bonsai?

Perhaps it is better to start by explaining what a bonsai is not. A bonsai is not a genetically dwarfed plant, it is not treated with magic potions to reduce its size and, above all, it is not kept small by cruelty in any way. In fact, given an adequate supply of water, air, light and nutrients, a properly maintained bonsai should outlive a full-size tree of the same species (see Light, Water and Air, pages 38–43).

Literally translated from Japanese, the term 'bonsai' means a tree in a pot. But over the centuries, the definition has come to mean a lot more. To begin with, the tree and the pot form a single harmonious unit where the shape, texture and colour of one complements the other. Then the tree must be shaped. It is not enough just to plant a tree in a pot and allow nature to take its course – the result would look nothing like a tree and would be very short-lived. Every branch and twig of a bonsai is shaped or eliminated until the chosen image is achieved. From then on, the image is maintained and improved by a constant regime of pruning and trimming.

At all times, a bonsai must be kept in perfect condition. A bonsai cannot outgrow an infestation of aphids in the same way a wild tree can. Nor can it send out long roots to search for water in periods of dry weather, and it doesn't receive a regular supply of nutrients from animals and decaying vegetation. A bonsai depends entirely on its current owner for all these things. But don't be deterred: it is not as difficult as it sounds. Remember the literal meaning of bonsai – a tree in a pot. Although a little more time-consuming, a modest bonsai should be no more difficult to care for than any other type of pot plant.

In the beginning…

Mankind has been growing plants in containers for thousands of years, normally for culinary or medicinal purposes and only very rarely for their beauty. When plants were containerized for decoration, it was because of their flowers or foliage. But on one occasion, probably in China, a new concept was born – that of creating miniature representations of natural landscapes in containers. Wall paintings dating back to the Han dynasty, around 200 BC, show such landscapes, complete with trees, rocks and grasses, being carried by servants. Nowadays, over 2,000 years later, these *penjing* still constitute a major part of bonsai culture in China and other Far-Eastern countries.

There are many legends about the spiritual significance of penjing, most involving powerful emperors or fiery dragons. One favourite suggests that an overweight emperor found travelling tiresome, so he demanded that a miniature replica of his empire should be built in his courtyard to enable him to survey his entire domain from the bedroom window. We shall never know the truth, but it certainly is true that for hundreds of years ownership of a miniature containerized landscape was a considerable status symbol.

The practice of growing single specimen trees in pots came later, again in China, but exactly when is a mystery. These early specimens displayed sparse foliage and rugged, gnarled trunks which often looked like animals or birds. These were called *pun-sai*, the root of the Japanese word *bonsai*, and were the forerunners of the million or more small, commercial 'indoor bonsai' exported from China each year.

The shape of the white pine bonsai and the decoration on the pot indicate the strong Chinese influence in Japanese culture in the late eighteenth century.

Bonsai in Japan

During the 11th and 12th centuries, there was considerable cultural movement between China and its neighbours, particularly with the Japanese who readily adopted much of Chinese art and philosophy. Perhaps the most significant influence was the Chinese Zen religion, whose monks played a leading role in introducing the art of bonsai to the Japanese ruling classes.

Bonsai rapidly became entrenched in Japanese culture and seems to have been practised on both a spiritual and an aesthetic level. While the Buddhist monks adopted the intellectual, abstract approach, there is considerable evidence that as early as the late 13th century stunted wild trees were collected and trained as bonsai by ordinary citizens. Specialist techniques also began to develop at this time, although, as the poet Yoshida Kenko suggested in his *Essays in Idleness, c.* 1330, the results were not always successful and tended towards deformity rather than beauty. He regarded bonsai as unnatural and once compared them to beggars with twisted limbs. The same argument continues to rage today, wherever bonsai are grown.

ABOVE A Japanese master at work.

BELOW This zelkova, otherwise known as the grey bark elm (*Zelkova serrata*), already looks like a miniature tree, yet it won't cost a fortune.

Development of modern bonsai

Like all leisure activities, bonsai has been subjected to changes in fashion over the years. For example, in the mid-17th century the passion was for camellias, then azaleas. Each year new varieties were exhibited at the equivalent of modern flower shows. One document records 162 new varieties of azalea and 200 camellias. At one point, the obsession with variegated plants was so strong that the artistic approach to bonsai was almost completely lost in the frantic search for new leaf patterns and colours.

However, it survived, and during the Edo period (1603–1868) became truly established as a highly refined artistic discipline. The techniques became ritualized and the shapes and placement of the branches and trunks governed by a very strict code. Several manuals were produced detailing the exact requirements of the ideal bonsai and giving extremely precise horticultural instructions.

By the late 19th century, bonsai had become an industry, with many professional artists and commercial growers supplying an ever-increasing demand at all levels of society. In 1892 the first Artistic Bonsai Concourse was held in a Tokyo restaurant, and in 1928 the first of the current series of Kokufu-ten exhibitions was held in the Metropolitan Art Museum in Tokyo.

ABOVE The Japanese characters for bonsai are still identical to the Chinese characters.

LEFT A specimen Japanese black pine in all its glory. Trees of this stature are quite expensive and are for serious collectors only!

Japanese and Chinese styles

While bonsai in Japan was undergoing centuries of development and refinement, which was producing increasingly simplified and, to the Westerner, arguably more aesthetic results, in China the only significant change was that bonsai became more populist in its appeal. There are a great number of myths and legends surrounding Chinese bonsai, and the grotesque or animal-like trunks and root formations are still highly prized today. Chinese bonsai come from the landscape of the imagination and images of fiery dragons and coiled serpents take far greater precedence over images of trees.

Classic Japanese bonsai follow clearly defined styles which are based on idealized images of natural tree forms. The story each one tells is of the tree itself and the environment in which it lives.

ABOVE The animal-like roots of this highly characterful sageretia are typical of Chinese specimen bonsai.

RIGHT This little pistachio would be a good, inexpensive tree for the novice to learn on.

Bonsai in the West

There are records of early Victorian travellers returning from the Orient telling stories of bizarre little trees with intentionally bent and twisted branches, apparently clinging to life in ceramic containers. But it was not until the Paris Exhibition in 1878 that bonsai were appreciated by the Western public. The display in the Japanese Pavilion won a gold medal and brought bonsai to the attention of the European middle classes.

Ironically, it was as a result of World War Two that bonsai became the internationally popular pastime it is today. Servicemen and diplomats returning from tours of duty in Japan brought back examples as souvenirs. Some people took time to learn about their care before leaving Japan and a few of these original imports are still alive today. In the United States, the large ex-patriot Japanese population in California provided the vital link between the energetic, enthusiastic Westerner and the traditional Japanese wisdom built up over the centuries.

Nowadays, bonsai is practised all over the world, and the different cultures, climates and

species of each country have prompted the development of new styles and techniques. The Port Jackson figs of Australia, the American buttonwood and the Scots pines of Europe all have distinct natural styles that are echoed in their bonsai forms and particular horticultural idiosyncrasies that have required the development of appropriate new techniques. Local clubs are formed by groups of enthusiasts, keen to help each other learn. Each year there are many local, national and international conventions and seminars where amateurs and professionals gather to exhibit their trees and increase their knowledge.

Commercial bonsai

For most of us, bonsai is not a quest for artistic fulfilment or a scientific challenge; it is simply a rewarding and creative pastime.

Our first encounter with bonsai was probably in a local garden centre or department store,

For centuries, potted trees, like the beautiful flowering apricots pictured here, have been used in China to greet visitors to family residences and important buildings.

where modest little trees are on sale for not-so-modest prices. Sadly, the high price seldom reflects a tree's artistic merit but more the fact that producing a bonsai is a time-consuming and labour-intensive operation, and then it has to be shipped halfway around the world!

Indoor bonsai

Ironically, although it was the Japanese who introduced bonsai to the West and first opened up the market here, the majority of commercial bonsai sold in the West today are produced in China. For one thing, there is no shortage of labour or space in China. But more importantly, the Chinese traditionally use sub-tropical or tropical species which, in temperate climates, need extra protection during winter.

A typical Japanese bonsai nursery, where plants are meticulously cared for and kept in perfect health.

Furthermore, unlike hardy species, they can be kept indoors all year round, making them ideally suited to flat-dwellers, and this way their appeal is broadened to the non-gardener.

The Chinese were very quick to seize the opportunity to exploit the West's growing fascination with bonsai and set up large-scale nurseries to produce vast quantities of relatively cheap trees. At this low end of the range, the plants are little more than two- or three-year-old rooted cuttings that have been hard pruned once to induce a mass of new shoots prior to export. One person can prune up to a thousand plants in a day.

Medium-priced Chinese bonsai may often feature a clay figure or pagoda glued to a stone somewhere in the pot, but this is just the producer's idea of what appeals to Westerners and should be discarded if not to your taste. The trees themselves, however, will have much more to offer. They are older, probably field-grown plants that have been hard pruned. The new growth is shaped with wire or ties and

allowed to grow for a season before being pruned again. Then they are regularly trimmed for another year or more before eventually being potted up ready for export.

As the trees increase in price, the true Chinese styles begin to emerge, and the more expensive specimens are likely to be truly authentic and full of Chinese magic. These are invariably collected from the wild, and can be extremely old. They are styled and refined for a number of years before being offered to overseas buyers. But even at this level, the Chinese make little effort to disguise the evidence of the hand of man. Saw cuts and pruned branches are allowed either to heal or to decay at nature's whim. It's as if the human intervention is just another episode in the tree's natural history.

Other Far-Eastern countries such as Taiwan and Korea are beginning to take large shares of the 'indoor' bonsai market, concentrating on the low-to medium-priced trees – older, specimen bonsai from these sources are rare. Mediterranean countries like Italy and Israel also produce small sub-tropical bonsai, mostly olives, pistachio, pomegranate and the like. These can be a source of interesting material on which to work but, size for size, rarely have the charm or character of Far-Eastern trees.

Outdoor bonsai

In spite of indoor bonsai's more popular appeal, once hooked the bonsai enthusiast invariably turns to hardy species. A collection of hardy bonsai, living in the open, rewards its owner with all the changes in colour and texture associated with the seasons. Your work schedule will also be dictated by the seasons, each tree telling you when the time is right. As outdoor bonsai mature, the bark develops fissures and the soil becomes covered in moss. Outdoor bonsai bring you closer to nature and introduce greater challenges and more possibilities, which is why they are preferred by the connoisseur.

Almost all hardy bonsai are produced in Japan. Generally, they are field-grown for between five and twenty years, sometimes even longer, but nowadays rarely collected from the wild; those that are tend to remain in Japan. While in the open ground, the trees receive some pruning and shaping before being lifted and examined. The trees with the most potential or the fewest imperfections are retained for further development and the rest are exported as cheap 'starter' trees.

The cycle is repeated, and each time the best are retained and the rest are exported at an appropriately higher price than the last batch. And at each successive cycle, the standard of workmanship and the time taken over aesthetic consideration is increased. The essence of Japanese bonsai is the quest for perfection and this system serves to maximize the artistic as well as the commercial potential of each particular tree.

TOP Thousands of *Acer palmatum* starter trees growing under protected conditions in a modern Japanese nursery.

ABOVE Driftwood-style bonsai created from wild plants collected from the mountains. These are increasingly rare and are now very expensive.

Buying a bonsai

Bonsai are traditionally expensive items, largely because they have to travel halfway around the world to reach you. In view of the high cost, it is particularly important to understand what you are buying, and make sure you get the best deal.

Buying a bonsai

Your first introduction to bonsai might well have been when you received one as a gift. If so, you are not alone. Almost half of all the imported tropical and sub-tropical bonsai are bought as gifts. On the other hand, you may have seen bonsai on display and decided that you want to try keeping your own. Either way, the fact that you are reading this book indicates that you are interested enough to learn more, and to acquire more bonsai.

High street bonsai

Bonsai have a reputation for being expensive which is often true. But you may not always get what you think you are paying for. Just before Christmas, so-called 'bonsai' crop up everywhere – street markets, garage forecourts, even car-boot sales and flea markets, and you should beware of all of these. Some such traders will, no doubt, offer good-quality products at a reasonable price, but they are a minority. Shop around and compare prices and general health.

Japanese bonsai properly displayed in a UK nursery, each tree receiving adequate light and air to keep it in a healthy condition.

Bear in mind that prices will fall in the January sales, making it a good time to buy.

Department stores also stock up with a number of indoor bonsai just before the Christmas rush. The better ones will offer trees recently imported from the Far East. They will have spent weeks in a dark container, then in a heated greenhouse, before winding up on the shelf. Most will be tough enough to recover if properly cared for, but generally in-store care is poor. Stores with a keener eye for an easy buck might offer minute, recently rooted cuttings in shallow pots, packed in carton boxes with a clear window. This keeps the plant green for a while, but the lack of light and fresh air weakens it tremendously. It is best not to buy these at all. If you do, you will be paying for the packaging which, if the plant is to survive, must be discarded immediately.

Mail order

Many specialist nurseries offer a mail-order service. They pack the trees well and generally use contract carriers for next-day delivery. If you are unable to get to a specialist nursery and you are happy buying a bonsai without seeing it, then mail order is worth a try. Check first whether or not the supplier offers a refund for trees damaged on arrival, and unpack the tree while the delivery man is still at the door.

Advertisements in consumer magazines for mail-order bonsai should always be regarded with the utmost suspicion.

Specialist nurseries

There is no doubt that specialist nurseries are far and away the best places to buy bonsai. They depend on year-round business and rely heavily on repeat customers, so they have to be good. Most are run by people who became hooked on bonsai and turned their hobby into a business. As such, they have a good knowledge of bonsai care which they are always happy to pass on. They also stock all the bonsai paraphernalia such as training wire, tools, pots, fertilizers and so on. Many will offer holiday care and 'hospital' facilities for sick trees. They may also offer a repotting and pruning service, but after reading this book you shouldn't need to call upon either!

Wherever you decide to buy your bonsai, you should first arm yourself with a little knowledge to enable you to choose a good buy.

Health

Bonsai spend weeks in a shipping container and six months in quarantine before being offered for sale. By the time they reach the sales benches, they should be in perfect condition. But, unlike plants in garden nurseries, bonsai can spend many months, or even years, waiting to be bought. With the best intentions in the world, some will inevitably contract various ailments or suffer from an unintentional lack of attention from time to time. Always check trees from the bottom upwards.

• *Gently* try to rock the trunk to see if the tree is secure in its pot. If it rocks easily, the roots are not completely filling the pot for some reason. This may mean that they are rotting or, at least, not growing well. Check that the drainage holes are adequate and are not blocked with roots. The presence of moss on the soil is a good sign, but water-loving plants like liverwort indicate poor soil conditions.

• Look for old wounds that were not sealed properly and may be decaying. This can be difficult to arrest and may eventually cause more serious problems.

• Dead shoots may be a normal reaction to the lack of light and air caused by congested foliage. In these cases, there is nothing to worry about, since the shoots will readily regenerate once the tree receives your attention. Dead branches, though, are another matter. The loss of a branch may be caused by wire constriction, disease, root ailments or mistreatment.

Tropical bonsai need to be kept in an artificial environment – in the nursery and in the home. At this nursery, the conditions are ideal for the health and vigour of the plants.

• Yellowing leaves can mean over- or under-watering, insufficient light or a deficiency of trace elements, particularly magnesium. All these are easily cured, but that should be the nursery's responsibility, not yours. Yellow leaves may also indicate more serious root problems, so try the trunk-rocking test.

• Dry areas of foliage can be caused by temporary conditions such as draught or drought. They may also be caused by infestations of spider mites. In either case, if the leaves have totally withered, the likelihood is that the shoots have done likewise and perhaps even the entire branch.

• Finally, check the foliage thoroughly for pests and evidence of fungal disease. Distorted or discoloured leaves are normally caused by one or the other problem. Fortunately, most are easily cured but, once again, this should be the nursery's job.

Shape

The most important thing is that you find the shape of your bonsai pleasing, but don't be fooled by a dense canopy of bright green leaves. Trees have an internal structure of trunk and branches that also needs to be examined. The standard of workmanship that has gone into shaping the tree will also affect its quality. As with the health check, start at the bottom.

• On outdoor bonsai, the roots should be evenly distributed around the trunk and should flare naturally as they enter the soil. Twisted, crossing or uneven visible roots are particularly ugly and generally impossible to rectify. On indoor trees, which follow the Chinese style,

A tangled root mass like this is inefficient and will require reorganizing if the plant is to progress.

Beware of poor grafts, especially on maples. The swelling will get worse as time passes.

the roots are normally intentionally exposed and randomly arranged. Here, the emphasis will be on the bizarre, but they should still appear natural.

• Many desirable varieties are grafted onto root stocks of a similar variety. Graft unions almost always leave a permanent scar and often swell, disfiguring the trunk. Poor graft unions become worse as time passes, not better. Japanese white pine (*Pinus parviflora*) are always grafted onto black pine (*Pinus thunbergii*) root stocks. The union is made just below the first branch to take advantage of the black pine's fissured bark. Normally, the first branch is trained to hide the graft union, so make sure this branch is healthy and does its job properly.

• Trunks have an infinite variety of shapes – on indoor trees, they may be coiled or dramatically bent back on themselves. On outdoor trees, they are more likely to follow conventional tree-like forms. In either case, the trunk should taper from base to apex and should be clear of branches for about the bottom third. It should also be completely free of ugly scars. With group or forest plantings, the trunks should be varied in height, thickness and spacing, and no one trunk should obscure another.

• Mass-produced bonsai are wire trained just like any other, and are often exported with the wire still on. This is not a problem in itself, but it is not uncommon to find that the wire has already begun to cut into the bark, causing spiral scars that will take many years to heal. Occasionally, you may find bonsai with wire deeply embedded in the bark and impossible to remove. Don't believe the myth that this is done to 'age' the tree artificially. It is the result of carelessness and nothing else.

• All bonsai are hard pruned at some point in their preparation for sale, and all pruning will leave a scar of some sort. When working on your own trees, carefully hollow out the wound and seal it (see page 60). However, this is not practical on a commercial scale, so short stubs are left which can be cut off and hollowed out when you get the tree home. Before you buy, consider how this could be done. A trunk that has been cut through at right angles to reduce height and induce branching will not only have an unnatural shape but the large scar will be a permanent feature. A good bonsai should either show no scars at all or should have all pruning wounds incorporated into the design, by carving them into natural-looking hollows or shaping and bleaching the stubs to create *jins* (see Keeping in trim, pages 58–69).

• The easiest way to learn how to assess the branch structure of a bonsai is to look at the full-size trees around you. On old conifers, the branches are horizontal or sweep downwards, and each bears wide, shallow pads of foliage. The branches become progressively shorter and thinner as they get higher up the trunk, giving the tree a conical shape. On deciduous trees, branches are horizontal or sweep gently upwards, frequently forking. Each branch bears a mass of foliage that forms part of the overall dome-shaped canopy. Branches are distributed evenly around the trunk. Making allowances for scale and the desire for an 'interesting' shape, the same principle applies to bonsai, albeit in a simplified way. Check for wire marks and ugly pruning scars. Also, avoid trees with two branches positioned immediately opposite each other. These 'bar branches' will jar the eye and in the future will cause the trunk to swell where they join it.

TOP Wire scars on branches or trunks weaken the tree and will take many years to heal.

ABOVE Trident maples readily form a strong buttress at the base of the trunk – a feature much prized in Japan.

Species

Before buying a bonsai, you must consider where it will be expected to live. If you want a tree for indoors, assess the light and temperature levels in the room and decide whether or not you can put the tree outside during summer. If you prefer outdoor bonsai, you need to consider the amount of sunlight your garden receives. Can you provide dappled shade all day or protection from the hot afternoon sun? The following pages provide a guide to the species that are suitable for various domestic environments.

Bright sunny rooms

Many modern homes have large picture-windows which allow in plenty of light. Windows which face the afternoon sun will also admit a lot of heat, the effect of which is amplified by the glass. Many species will suffer in these conditions, and should be kept away from the direct sun but close enough to the window to receive good light. Don't keep your trees on the windowsill because at night the temperature close to the glass can fall dramatically, particularly in winter when the central heating is off. This constant extreme temperature fluctuation can be fatal to tropical and sub-tropical bonsai. Positioning trees some distance from the window will reduce the strength of the sunlight and broaden the range of species that you can grow successfully.

Podocarpus love bright, warm conditions and will thrive close to a large, sunny window in a centrally heated flat.

Suitable species
• Bamboo
• Bougainvillea
• Chinese elm
• Chinese yew
• Jasmine orange
• Lagerstroemia
• Olive
• Pistachio
• Pomegranate
• Privet
• Serissa

Dull rooms

North- or east-facing rooms may appear quite dull, but in a position close to the window there will be sufficient light to keep several species perfectly happy.

One solution to the problem of low natural light is to install purpose-built artificial lighting for your bonsai collection. This is not as costly or impractical as it might at first seem. Although there are a number of horticultural lighting systems on the market, ordinary blue-white fluorescent strip lighting provides the complete spectrum of light needed by most species, and is cheap to run. The drawback is that the light is of fairly low intensity. Ideally, the strips should be positioned 20–30 cm (8–12 in) from the foliage. Use three strips, positioning two directly above the trees – one towards the front and another further back – and the third lower down, behind the trees. Keep the lights on for seven to ten hours a day and rotate the trees through 90 degrees every few days to ensure that all parts receive adequate light. The lights generate slight heat which can also benefit the trees, but the drying effect of this needs to be countered by regular spraying and extra vigilance when watering.

Suitable species
• Carmona
• Cycad
• Fig
• Myrtle
• Nandina
• Sageretia

BELOW Ficus are tough plants that are accustomed to the shadier, more humid conditions below taller trees.

Sunny gardens

In mid-summer, the heat from the afternoon sun is reflected off fences, buildings and patios, sending the local temperature soaring. Pots heat up and dry out rapidly. The sunlight is intense and can itself be damaging, particularly in recent years, when its harmful rays are not so efficiently filtered by the atmosphere. Some species, especially when grown in pots, dislike such intense, hot sun; others positively love it. But all bonsai should have their pots shaded or regularly cooled with water during very hot spells in order to prevent the roots from becoming too hot and cooking. Erecting a purpose-built shaded area will enable you to grow a wider range of species.

Chinese junipers are adapted to life on exposed mountains where they receive full sun. Providing similar conditions in your garden will keep the foliage compact.

Suitable species
• Celtis
• Chinese elm
• Chinese juniper
• Cotoneaster
• Crab apple
• Flowering quince
• Japanese black pine
• Japanese cedar
• Japanese holly
• Japanese white pine
• Needle juniper
• Pyracantha
• Wisteria

Shaded gardens

In many ways, a shaded garden offers the ideal environment for bonsai, provided the sky directly above your bonsai is not obscured by overhanging trees and the sun is reflected off a wall or fence into the garden for at least part of the day to maintain seasonal temperatures. Even species that prefer full sun will do quite nicely with good overhead light, although the growth might be a little 'leggy'. This can be controlled by reducing the nitrogen in the feeding programme and regular trimming.

The foliage, flowers and coloured bark of stewartia all perform best in shadier conditions.

Suitable species
- Azalea
- Beech
- Chinese yew
- Cypress
- Ginkgo
- Hornbeam
- Japanese maple
- Stewartia
- Trident maple
- Zelkova

How a tree works

It is easy enough to carry out the instructions that follow in relation to watering, feeding and pruning, but knowing and understanding something about how trees function will greatly increase your enjoyment of bonsai and give you more confidence in caring for your trees.

Roots

Because the roots are out of sight, it is very easy to overlook the importance of a healthy, vigorous root system. More often than not, when a bonsai begins to look sickly it is an indication of some form of root disorder.

Roots have three functions. First of all, they provide anchorage, holding the tree firm in the ground. In the wild, they do this by growing in all directions and eventually thickening to form a buttress at the base of the trunk. Secondly, they absorb moisture and soluble nutrients from the soil. Thirdly, they store sugars during dormancy in order to provide energy for the first flush of growth in spring. Let's look at these functions in more detail.

Anchorage

This may seem rather irrelevant to bonsai, but in fact the roots are still responsible for holding the tree firm in the pot. You will see in the section on repotting (see page 48) that wire can be used initially to hold the tree firmly, but this is unsightly and is therefore only temporary. If the roots lack vigour or are decaying, they will not fill the pot and the trunk will rock in the wind or as you work on the tree. This causes further damage to the roots, and so the vicious circle continues.

To hold a tree firm in its pot, the roots must be distributed all around the trunk and must grow sideways rather than downwards. One-sided root systems are unstable and will most likely also result in a one-sided branch structure. Roots that grow steeply downwards before spreading sideways tend to rely more on fine roots to provide anchorage.

Absorbing water and nutrients

Healthy, growing roots show plump and white at the tips. This is the most active part of the root system. The very tip is protected as it thrusts its way through the soil by a hard cap, which is constantly being worn away and

replaced. Behind this, the white part of the root is clothed in minute root hairs, which are composed of a single cell and can be almost invisible to the naked eye. Although water can be absorbed by older parts of the root, it is through these root hairs that the water and, most importantly, nutrients are more readily absorbed due to their enormous combined surface area. Root hair production is stimulated by moisture and oxygen present in the soil.

Absorption of water takes place by the process of osmosis. The membranes surrounding root cells are semi-permeable, which means that they have millions of tiny pores just big enough to allow one water molecule to pass through. When the concentration of nutrient salts inside the root

The plump, white growing tips indicate a healthy and vigorous root system.

is greater than immediately outside, water molecules pass through the pores into the root hairs to dilute the solution. This means that the solution of salts in the root hairs is now weaker than in the adjacent cell, so water molecules pass one cell further into the root, and so on. Once the water has reached the xylem cells in the core of the root, it is drawn up the tree by capillary action.

The pores in the semi-permeable membrane are big enough to allow water molecules to pass but not dissolved nutrients. These are absorbed electrochemically. All the chemicals in question are either positively or negatively charged. When the tree requires a particular nutrient – say, potash – which is positively charged, the root expels a positively charged hydrogen ion to make way for it. Simultaneously, one pore changes size and shape to allow just one potassium ion through into the root.

Nobody is sure how the tree can judge its nutrient requirements so precisely, but this remarkable microscopic process takes place hundreds of millions of times a day.

Root burn

If the concentration of salts outside the roots is greater than that inside, the osmosis is reversed and water passes out of the roots back into the soil to equalize the solutions. The tree will wilt and begin to shed young shoots. This is why you should never use fertilizers in excess of the recommended rates or when the roots are inactive. Similarly, feeding directly after repotting, when there are few, if any, root hairs, can have a similar effect. Regular prolonged watering to flush the soil clean of residual salts is a wise precaution.

Nutrient storage

Older, thicker roots develop bundles of sap-conducting cells called the phloem, which are also present in the trunk and branches. These cells conduct the sugars from the leaves and

The spreading roots on this azalea look like fingers grasping the soil. This type of root structure is efficient as well as imparting strength and character to the tree.

distribute them to all parts of the plant wherever they are needed for growth, including the roots. In late summer and autumn, when growth slows down and eventually ceases, the phloem becomes plump with excess sugars, which are stored there until they are needed to support new growth in spring. Transplanting trees and pruning roots in autumn causes considerable loss of stored sugars which will retard spring growth. This is why you should wait until the buds begin to swell, which indicates that at least some of the stored sugars have been returned to the growing points, before pruning the roots. The exceptions are some flowering plants that seem to produce even more flowers and fruit if given a hard time and repotted in autumn.

Trunks and branches

The main purpose of the trunk and branches of a tree is purely structural, that is to support as much foliage as possible in positions where it will receive the most light and air. They also, naturally, have to conduct water, nutrients and sugars from the roots to the leaves and back. In a mature tree, most of the tissue forming the trunk and branches – the heartwood – is dead. It has become lignified (literally, turned into wood) and hardened, and is responsible for the tree's strength. Naturally, the thicker the heartwood, the more difficult it is to bend. The actual living part of the trunk and branches is confined to the outermost layers, and it is here that all the activity takes place.

ABOVE The broad, spreading foliage pads of this cedar of Lebanon are typical of ancient conifers and provide inspiration for the bonsai artist.

LEFT Deciduous trees such as this maple reward you with year-round interest as they change in response to the seasons.

The cambium

If you gently scratch a twig with your fingernail, you will notice a bright green layer just below the surface. This is the cambium – a single layer of cells surrounding the trunk, branches and shoots. The cambium is constantly developing new cells of different types, on both the inside and the outside, throughout the growing season. It also has the ability to initiate new buds or new roots, as well as to fuse with the cambium of another plant, such as in the process of grafting.

When a thick branch is cut through during the growing season, the cambium has a heyday. It responds to the loss of a branch by generating a mass of completely new shoots that emerge like a crown from between the bark and the sapwood in an attempt to replace the lost foliage. Most of these shoots will die off through overcrowding and lack of light, but the strongest will continue to grow vigorously.

The cambium is also responsible for producing the healing tissue that 'rolls' over wounds. If you look closely at a recent pruning cut, you can see how this tissue emerges from between the bark and the wood.

The xylem

On the inside of the cambium, the new cells it produces form the xylem, which conducts the water upwards. It is the formation of new xylem each year that creates the familiar annual rings. The xylem remains active for a year or more, depending on the species, and while active forms what is referred to as sapwood. This is the lighter-coloured group of rings surrounding the heartwood. The rate of a tree's growth and the pattern of its xylem cells determine the strength and grain of its wood.

The production of new xylem is also what makes branches set in position when trained with wire. Once the tensile strength of the new xylem is sufficient to counter that of the old wood, the wire may be removed and the branch will stay in place. The wood in young shoots and branches is composed entirely of xylem, which is malleable and will readily adopt new shapes. Older branches that contain heartwood take longer to set. The tensions created by bending the branch will always be present, and even if a branch appears to have set, it may well gradually move back towards its original position as the soft xylem yields under pressure from the tough heartwood.

The phloem

On the outside of the cambium, the new cells form the phloem, which distributes the sugars manufactured by the leaves to all other parts of the plant. As old phloem cells are replaced by new ones each year, they in turn harden and become the bark. As the years pass, the bark thickens and in most cases becomes corky and flakes, peels or develops fissures. The precise formation of phloem cells and the length of their useful lives differs between one species and another. This explains why different trees display their own unique characteristic bark patterns as they mature.

Why bonsai live so long

In the wild, a healthy tree will continue growing until it reaches its genetically predetermined height. Once this has been achieved, the crown begins to spread sideways, generally forming a dome. Eventually, the distance between the active roots at the periphery of the root system and the increasing mass of foliage at the tips of the branches becomes too great and the tree begins to deteriorate. As the foliage receives less water and fewer nutrients from the roots, it is therefore less able to supply adequate sugars to generate new roots and the tree eventually dies.

Trees that are regularly pruned, such as pollards or hedgerow trees, live for much longer than their full-size counterparts because they never reach their maximum dimensions. They will not die of old age until the structural heartwood rots and collapses.

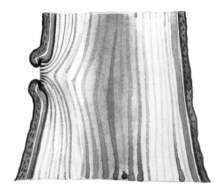

TOP Each year a new layer of wood is formed which gradually 'rolls' over wounds until they are completely healed.

ABOVE When thick branches are pruned, masses of new shoots emerge from the cambium layer, between the bark and the sapwood. Most of these will die off through overcrowding and only the strongest will continue to grow.

Because a bonsai is constantly being encouraged, by pruning, to produce new healthy roots and shoots, it is always actively growing, trying to reach maturity. The actual living part – the cambium, flanked by the xylem and the phloem – is never more than a few years old. Provided enough growth takes place each year to lay down sufficient new xylem and phloem to sustain the tree, a bonsai will always remain essentially young and should, in theory at least, live for ever.

A waxy coating on the needles of conifers protects them against frost and snow.

A waxy coating on thick, leathery leaves protects against the hot sun and also conserves moisture.

Leaves

Each leaf converts water from the soil and carbon dioxide from the air into essential sugars in a process called photosynthesis. Without sufficient light, the leaves lose much of their green chlorophyll, the substance that enables photosynthesis to take place, consequently losing their ability to function.

Some shade is preferable for almost all plants grown in containers, but deep shade will cause problems, as will excessive sun. Too much sun, although providing the necessary light, will cause the leaves to overheat. They will rapidly close their breathing pores (stomata) in order to reduce water evaporation. This causes the leaf to 'shut down' until the sun becomes less intense. During this time, the leaf is not manufacturing sugars because the process relies on a constant passage of water through the leaf and a supply of carbon dioxide, which is absorbed through the same stomata.

Leaf types

Plants that normally live in semi-shade, such as azaleas and Japanese maples, have delicate, thin-skinned leaves that easily become brown and withered if grown in full sun or exposed to drying winds. Plants that are exposed to the hot sun have thick, leathery leaves, often with a waxy coating that helps prevent water evaporation. A waxy coating is also used by species that prefer extremely cold conditions. Most conifers have waxy leaves to protect them from the cold and to prevent snow and frost forming on the needles.

The variety of leaf colour and shape is vast, and makes collecting different species fascinating. The size can also vary considerably, even within the same variety, depending on the growing conditions of the individual plant. Plants growing in semi-shade will bear large, deep green leaves. The same variety growing in a small bonsai pot in full sun will have much smaller leaves, which will not display the same richness of colour.

Buds

On most species, there is a tiny, embryonic bud at the base of each leaf stalk (petiole). As the bud opens in spring, the central core elongates to form the shoot, with leaves distributed at intervals (internodes) along its length. As it extends, the bud at the growing tip is constantly undergoing a cycle of opening, extension and regeneration. If this is removed, the energy will be diverted into the next one or two buds back down the shoot.

Each bud is surrounded by scales, which can be anything from green, through browns to bright red, depending on the species. The scales are designed to protect the delicate, partly formed leaves in the bud from the sun, rain, frost and insect attack. They are, in fact, modified leaves and also have embryonic buds at the base of each scale. This explains why a mass of new shoots emerges from the short stub left when hard pruning current year's growth.

Buds can also be formed on old wood in reaction to more severe pruning or to some other trauma, such as drought or an attack of fungal disease. The cambium layer works to regenerate lost foliage by rapidly developing new buds that force their way through the bark. These are called adventitious buds and can appear on branches, trunks and even on old roots near the surface of the soil. In bonsai cultivation, the production of adventitious buds is of key importance because they are selectively used to grow new shoots to replace outgrown or congested areas of foliage.

As the tree begins to stir from its dormancy in spring, the buds start to swell. Tiny, pale-coloured lines appear at the edge of each scale as they begin to separate. This indicates an increase in root activity and signals the time for repotting before growth is too far advanced.

Autumn colour

One of the most rewarding aspects of trees is their vivid autumn coloration, varying from bright yellow through reds to purple. Many of

RIGHT **This magnified bud reveals a tightly compressed mass of embryonic leaves, complete with stem and another terminal bud.**

LEFT **The upper surface of a leaf absorbs sunlight, which helps convert water and carbon dioxide into nourishing sugars. The underside contains the pores – stomata – through which the plant breathes.**

these pigments are in the leaves when the shoots emerge from the buds, but are masked by the presence of chlorophyll. Other pigments are the result of chemical changes that take place in early autumn. As autumn approaches, the leaves cease producing sugars and the chlorophyll breaks down and is reabsorbed.

Autumn colour can be enhanced by keeping your trees in a warm, sunny spot during the day in late summer and early autumn but as cold as possible at night. This maximizes the colour-forming breakdown of substances during the day, but their redistribution to other parts of the plant is hindered by the night-time cold.

Don't worry if your bonsai lose their leaves before full-sized trees lose theirs. This is quite common and, although disappointing, does no harm.

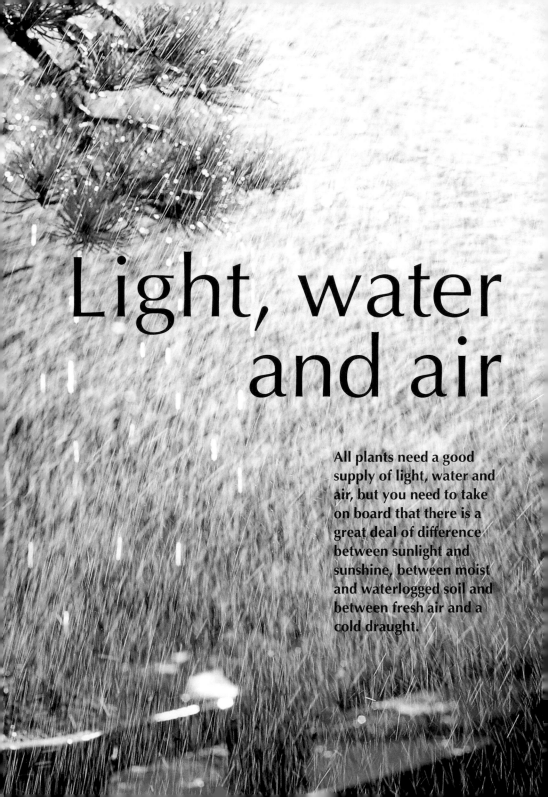

Light, water and air

All plants need a good supply of light, water and air, but you need to take on board that there is a great deal of difference between sunlight and sunshine, between moist and waterlogged soil and between fresh air and a cold draught.

Light

As we saw in the previous chapter, leaves
need a certain amount of sunlight in order to
photosynthesize and nourish the plant with
sugars. In over-shady conditions, leaves will
grow larger to gather as much light as possible
and the internodes (distances between the
leaves) will increase as the plant tries to extend
shoots rapidly to reach through the overhead
canopy to the sun. In good light, leaves will be
smaller and internodes much shorter. If the sun
is too strong, however, many plants will throw
out new growths from close to the trunk, where
they are shaded by the scorched outer foliage.
Many plants also use day length, rather than
temperature, to trigger seasonal phases such
as flowering or leaf-fall.

Bearing in mind, of course, that different
species prefer different amounts of sunlight, it
is important to learn a little about the natural
habitat of the full-size cousins of your bonsai.

Insufficient light causes the shoots to become leggy
and the internodes (spaces between the leaves) to
extend out of proportion to the tree.

Pines and junipers that are found growing on
exposed mountainsides are naturally adapted
to tolerate full sun. Indeed, growth can be
rather disappointing in shady conditions.
When positioned close to a wall, a bonsai pine
or juniper will grow vigorously on the open
side, but may even start to die back on the
shaded side.

On the other hand, if you keep a maple or an
azalea, both plants of woodland margins and
valleys, in an exposed situation, the side away
from the sun will produce much healthier and
more vigorous growth. The leaves of red maples
will hold their colour for longer if kept in semi-
shade, although returning them to full sun in
autumn will greatly intensify seasonal colour.

In bonsai, we try to strike a happy medium.
Few people can provide perfect conditions for
all species, but most can find a sunny corner
or erect some shade netting. Your bonsai isn't
going to die through too much or too little
sunlight, but it will tell you that it's not happy.

One final point. Remember to turn each
bonsai through 90 degrees every few days, so
that each area of foliage receives an equal
amount of light.

Delicate leaves, such as those on Japanese maples,
are easily scorched if exposed to drying winds.

Water

Surprisingly, more bonsai – or any other type of pot plant – are lost through overwatering than through drought. Very few species can tolerate permanently saturated soil and some prefer dry roots for part of the year (see the Tree Directory, pages 70–117, for details). But most require soil that is never allowed to dry out completely between waterings. If you are not sure whether your trees need watering, gently scratch away the surface of the soil to see how damp it is underneath. If it is just damp, then you can apply water; if it is wet, then leave it alone. If the soil is bone dry, water immediately using the immersion technique described on page 42. After a while, you should be able to judge how wet the soil is simply by the weight of the pot.

Coloured foliage can become green if light levels are too low. The upper leaves here remain red while those they are shading are beginning to turn green.

Water quality

Rainwater is by far the best for all plants, even in these days of acid rain. However, it is not always possible to collect sufficient rainwater to last more than a week or so in high summer. Storing large quantities of water for a long time has its dangers too. Air-borne spores of fungi such as phytopthera can enter the tank and, when watered into the pot, will attack the roots of your bonsai. Always keep water barrels tightly closed, and flush them out regularly with disinfectant and clean tap water.

Some species – known as calcifuges – do not tolerate lime, which may cause problems in areas where the tap water is 'hard' or rich in lime. Using an acid, organic-based soil and giving regular applications of a proprietary soil acidifier will counteract hard water. In extreme cases, exposed roots may become encrusted with lime deposit, which is harmless but unsightly. This can be removed with a stiff toothbrush. Never use artificially 'softened' water. Water softeners replace the calcium with sodium, which is even worse.

Tap water contains all manner of added chemicals that are designed to 'purify' it, or to strengthen our teeth and so on. None of these chemicals is particularly harmful to plants in low concentrations. However, occasionally higher than normal quantities of chlorine are introduced, particularly when water supplies are low or are drawn from rivers and the weather is warm. If you allow the water to stand in an open container for a few hours before use, the chlorine will evaporate.

Allowing the water to stand also brings it to the ambient temperature. Applying ice-cold water to a sun-warmed pot can shock the root system and cause temporary damage to the delicate growing tips. On the other hand, water that is a few degrees cooler than the roots will

Poorly drained soil will rapidly compact and become waterlogged. In soil like this, the tree's roots cannot breathe and will soon begin to rot.

refresh them and cool them down on hot days. The trick is to water either in the early morning or in the evening, when the roots are not so overheated. If you have a large collection of bonsai, you may choose to use a hose with a fine spray attachment. But remember that if a hose is left lying in the sun, the water in it will become very hot, so always let the water run for a few minutes before using it on your trees.

Overhead watering

The most natural way for a plant to receive water is from above. If your bonsai are properly potted – with the free-draining soil level just below the rim – this method should never cause a problem, but there are a few points to watch. Use a fine rose spray attachment to your hose or watering can. Excessive force will wash away the surface of the soil and tend to compact the rest. Fill the space between the soil surface and the rim with water and allow it to completely soak in, then repeat the process. By this time, water should be emerging from the drainage holes. If no water emerges after two applications, it may mean that the soil is too compacted or in poor condition, or perhaps the drainage holes are blocked. Unblock the holes and, in future, use the immersion watering technique described on the right until you can repot the tree at the earliest appropriate time.

Make sure you water the whole soil surface. The area behind the trunk is frequently neglected and this can weaken the roots in that area as well as the branches directly above them. Avoid the temptation to give all your bonsai the same amount of water every day. Check the pots individually every few days and adjust the watering as necessary.

Don't water in full sun unless the water has been allowed to stand for an hour or two. The leaves will enjoy being wetted at watering time provided that they are not in full sun. If you are using foliar feeds, or if the water is particularly hard, powdery deposits may appear on the foliage. These will wash off when it next rains.

Immersion watering

When bonsai trees are pot-bound, the roots become so dense that water is very slow to penetrate. You may see water running from the drainage holes, but this may have merely trickled between the soil and the pot, without wetting the soil at all. Imported indoor bonsai are generally planted in dense, clay-like soils, which may be fine in the growing nursery but are not appropriate for long-term use in domestic conditions. The soil becomes very compacted and is reluctant to absorb water. Furthermore, the soil is frequently mounded up above the rim of the pot so that the water just runs off before it has had a chance to soak in. In these cases, the immersion technique can get you and your bonsai out of trouble.

Place the bonsai in a bowl or bath and slowly add water until it covers the soil surface completely. You should see bubbles rising from the soil as the water replaces the air in the soil. If no bubbles appear, it may be because the soil is very compacted. Wait until the bubbles have stopped rising (or for half an hour if there were no bubbles), then remove the pot from the water. Tilt the pot to drain off excess water.

Immersing the entire pot in water every so often drives out all the stale air and ensures that there are no persistent dry spots. When the bubbles stop rising, the pot can be removed from the water and allowed to drain.

Automatic watering

Many commercial plant nurseries use a variety of automatic watering systems ranging from overhead sprays to individual drip feeds. These are fine if you want to maintain a large number of virtually identical plants, but are not so reliable when each plant requires more individual attention. Some experienced bonsai growers use timed low-level sprays or drip feeds while they are away from home, but they need extremely careful planning. The best advice is not to use automatic systems at all.

Air

Like people, trees need fresh air in order to remain healthy. Poor air circulation, either around the leaves and branches or around the roots (see page 46), will result in poor, sickly growth and creates ideal conditions for fungal and bacterial spores to take hold. Indoor bonsai that spend their lives in centrally heated, smoke-filled rooms will suffer just as badly as humans. The only difference is that the effect will be much more pronounced. Inner shoots will wither, leaves will become covered in powdery mildew, insects will colonize the foliage and the soil and trunk will become covered in algae.

Yellowing leaves may seem to be caused by dry soil but, more often than not, they result from overwatering or draughts.

To maintain good air circulation, indoors or outdoors, bonsai should be placed at about waist height, preferably on their own stand indoors or on slatted benches outside. This allows air of ambient temperature to circulate freely around all parts of the tree. Indoors, If placed lower, the air will be cooler than room temperature; if placed higher, it will be warmer and drier. Outdoors, trees that are placed too low will not only be short-changed as far as fresh air is concerned, but they will also be prey to snails, slugs and, worst of all, cats!

However, there is a big difference between fresh air circulation and draughts. A draught is a fast-moving current, usually colder than the surrounding air. Its effect can be devastating, causing rapid yellowing and shedding of leaves and die-back of young shoots. The pot cools down rapidly, restricting root growth.

Outdoors, strong winds can tear at the foliage, which not only disfigures the leaves but also reduces their efficiency. Even moderate winds can have a severe drying effect, which is as dangerous during winter as it is in summer. Species that are adapted to live in the relative protection of woodland margins or sheltered valleys, such as azaleas, Japanese maples and hornbeams, will develop brown edges to the leaves if exposed to winds.

Automatic watering systems ensure that an even amount of water is supplied to every plant, but they take no account of each plant's individual watering needs.

Life in a pot

When confined to a pot, a tree is unable to seek out sources of either water or nutrients. It cannot grow faster to beat an infestation of pests or to reach the sun. Its delicate roots and leaves can become bone dry in a matter of hours or can gradually suffocate in waterlogged soil. Your bonsai relies on you for its entire life support.

Soil

Ironically, your worst enemy is not drought but root decay, caused by overwatering or poor drainage. For this reason, it is essential to use a soil that is very free-draining. When you water the soil, the water should not lie on the surface. It should pass directly through the soil and begin flowing from the drainage holes within half a minute or so. This type of soil also prevents waterlogging even after prolonged rainfall.

Water retention

As well as being free-draining, a soil must be able to hold sufficient water to satisfy the tree's needs until the next watering. A soil containing fine particles, such as most garden soil, retains water but soon becomes compacted and impedes drainage. It is, therefore, necessary to use larger particles of water-retaining material – either organic or mineral.

Air spaces

Roots also need to 'breathe' in order to function efficiently and the micro-organisms that help them digest nutrients also require oxygen. Compacted soil or soil composed of particles that fit closely together will not contain enough air spaces to maintain healthy roots. Under these conditions, the helpful bacteria will perish and damaging anaerobic bacteria, which promote root decay, will thrive.

Which soil?

Japanese bonsai growers invariably use a commercial soil called Akadama. It is a hard, coarse, clay-like soil that has a natural granular structure with particles ranging from 1–5 mm ($\frac{1}{16}$–$\frac{1}{4}$ in). It holds water but has excellent drainage and contains ample air spaces. Although it can be fairly expensive in the West, experienced enthusiasts are increasingly turning to Akadama soil because of its unique properties, using it neat or mixing it with grit or sand for pines and drought-adapted species.

Japanese Akadama soil is perfect for most bonsai, but can be quite expensive.

Organic matter (leaf mould or peat) is the water-retaining ingredient in a home-made bonsai soil.

Grit or sharp sand is another basic ingredient for a home-made bonsai soil.

Proprietary potting composts are intended for houseplants growing in deep pots, which require far less frequent watering and are not expected to live as long as a bonsai. Moreover, most houseplants are perennials or, at most, sub-shrubs, which are not so particular as trees. These composts will rapidly compact and become waterlogged in shallow containers and therefore should not be used unless properly prepared (see opposite).

Many nurseries market their own 'bonsai soils', which vary greatly in quality. They use ingredients that are readily available to the amateur and the soils are seldom prepared with as much care as you might take when preparing your own. This is not carelessness, but the time-consuming sifting out of fine particles and the resulting waste is simply not cost-effective. To get the best from your bonsai, use Akadama or mix your own soil.

Grit and organic matter (see opposite) are mixed in equal parts to form an open, water-retentive but free-draining soil.

Proprietary soil improvers, such as this calcined clay, or crushed pumice, can be added to the mix to ensure that it remains absorbent and free-draining over time.

Mixing your own soil

A good, reliable, basic bonsai soil consists of just two ingredients: organic matter and grit.

Water retention is provided by organic matter such as peat, leaf mould, composted bark and so on. This should not be so far decomposed that it crumbles to dust when dry. Ideally, if moist organic matter is squeezed tightly in the hand, it should spring apart again when the pressure is released. Garden compost and farmyard manure are too rich in nutrients for the delicate, freshly pruned roots and often contain bacterial or fungal diseases. Whatever organic matter you choose, expect to discard at least 60 per cent in the sifting process.

All lumps larger than 5 mm (¼ in) should first be either broken up or removed. The remainder must then be scrupulously sifted to remove all particles smaller than 2 mm (⅟₁₆ in). Sift when the material is just damp.

An open, free-draining and well-ventilated structure is ensured by the addition of grit or coarse sand. This must also be sifted to retain particles from 2–5 mm (⅟₁₆–¼ in), or 2–3 mm (⅟₁₆–⅛ in) in smaller pots. Use only horticultural grit or sand. Under no circumstances use fresh builders' sand, which often contains impurities that can be extremely harmful to plants.

River sand is best because the grains are rounded so, even when fully settled, they don't fit tightly together. This ensures ample drainage and air spaces. Crushed granite or flint is easier to obtain and will do the job well, but the grains have flat sides that can fit close together. To counter this, use a more stable organic material such as composted bark rather than soft peat or leaf mould. On no account use beach sand, which contains salt, oil and other fatal impurities that are difficult to remove.

Finally, mix the two ingredients in roughly equal proportions. It is best to do this while the organic matter is still slightly damp. Store unused soil in a sealed plastic sack.

For species that require a more free-draining soil, such as those that are adapted to live in mountains or dry areas, you can add more coarse grit (see the Tree Directory, pages 70–117, for details). For added water retention, it is best to avoid the temptation to add more organic matter, but reduce the aggregate particle size of the grit to 2–3 mm (⅟₁₆–⅛ in). Alternatively, you can replace some of the grit with one of the proprietary granular soil conditioners on the market.

Soil conditioners

In recent years, a variety of soil conditioners have been developed for professional greenkeepers and gardeners. These include crushed pumice, baked or calcined clay and various other mineral composites. They are all available in suitable particle sizes and have the advantage of retaining their structures indefinitely. They can be added to the basic mix to increase water retention without impeding drainage. Some growers have achieved success by substituting all organic matter with pumice or calcined clay, controlling the amount of water retained by adjusting the proportion of grit.

Having prepared your basic mix, you may have to adjust it to the particular requirements of some species. Details of variations to the mix are given in the Tree Directory, pages 70–117.

Repotting

We have already seen how necessary it is
to maintain a constant cycle of regenerating
young, active roots in order to keep a bonsai
healthy and long-lived. This is achieved by
periodically repotting the tree and pruning
the roots. This process may seem 'cruel' to the
uninitiated, but it is, in fact, highly beneficial
to the tree if carried out properly.

When to repot

Detailed advice on the frequency of repotting
for individual species is given in the Tree
Directory, pages 70–117. But as a general rule,
young or small bonsai require repotting every
two or three years; older and larger specimens
less often. Signs that a tree needs repotting
include slow passage of water through the soil,
slowing of growth or roots that appear like a
coconut-fibre mat when the tree is eased from
the pot. On the other hand, if you remove a
tree from its pot after several years and see no
roots at the edge of the soil mass, something is
wrong. In such a case, all the old soil should be
thoroughly washed from the roots and replaced
with fresh, open soil at the earliest appropriate
time. Keep watering to a minimum and use
only foliar feeds until this can be done.

The best time of year to prune the roots is
in late winter to early spring, just as the buds
begin to swell slightly. This indicates that the
roots are also becoming active and will
therefore regenerate rapidly. It is not possible
to state a precise time for repotting – only close
observation of the tree can tell you when the
time is right, because each season is different
and plants begin to stir in a different sequence
from one year to another. However, generally
speaking, deciduous species should be repotted
first, and conifers up to a month later.

Repotting can be carried out during
autumn – most traditional gardeners would
recommend this time of year – but if you repot
in autumn the pruned roots will have to endure

Begin to ease the tree from its pot by gently tilting
it to one side. Never pull directly upwards as this
will damage the thicker roots.

the rigours of winter before they can begin to
heal. There is a considerable risk that the roots
will die back and decay after autumn repotting,
so such trees need to be kept frost-free and
watered minimally until spring.

How to repot

1 First, gently ease the tree from its pot. If the pot
has a lip on the inside of the rim, you may need
to use a sharp knife to cut around the edge of the
root mass before removing it. If the root mass is
stubborn, try pushing it out with a stick passed
through the drainage holes. Avoid pulling the
trunk too hard as this can strain the roots.

Using a metal hook, knitting needle or
similar, begin to 'comb' away the roots and soil.
Start at the edge and work all round, untangling
the roots as you go. Always draw the hook
outwards, not across the soil surface, otherwise
you may scar valuable surface roots. Take your
time and avoid tearing at the roots.

When combing the roots, work from the centre outwards, and take your time – rushing the job will damage heavy roots.

In ideal conditions, a bonsai will produce masses of fine feeding roots. Holding the tree up to allow the thinner roots to hang down, use sharp scissors to cut them back.

Continue to trim back the fine roots until the remaining root mass is about 1–2 cm (½–¾ in) smaller all round than the inside of the pot, as well as the depth.

Thoroughly clean the pot before securing the drainage mesh with wire. Some pots have special holes for the retaining wires. If yours doesn't, pass the wires through the drainage holes.

Add a thin drainage course of grit, then a layer of fresh soil at least 1 cm (½ in) thick. Mound the soil slightly where the trunk will sit.

Settle the tree in position and secure it by pulling the retaining wires over the roots and twisting them together until the tree is held firm. Be careful not to twist the wires too tightly.

2 Once you have untangled all the roots around the edge, you can begin to comb out the underside of the root mass, again working from the centre outwards. Give the tree a gentle shake every so often to remove loose soil. Continue untangling the roots until about half of the soil has been removed from around the edge and the base of the trunk has been exposed underneath. This latter point is extremely important, otherwise the tree will gradually 'rise' in the pot at each successive repotting.

3 At this stage, it is a good idea to spray the roots, firstly to keep them moist and secondly to wash away all soil residue so that you can get a better view of the root structure, which will help when you begin the process of pruning. I have now adopted the policy of washing away all old soil with a hose every second or third repotting. This not only ensures fresh, healthy soil right up to the trunk and removes any undesirable organisms, but it also enables me to examine the whole root system for signs of decay and to improve its structure by accurate selective pruning.

4 Now you can begin to prune the roots. Use a very sharp tool. If you have washed away all the loose soil, the tool will retain its edge; if you haven't, the grit clinging to the roots will soon blunt it. Begin by pruning all the thick roots that have grown to the edge of the pot. Cut these back by between a third and a half, cutting back the thickest roots the furthest. You will remove a certain amount of fine feeding roots in the process, but new ones will grow from around the pruning cuts.

5 Hold the tree up and allow the remaining thinner roots to hang freely. These must now be trimmed with sharp scissors. If there are masses of fine roots, they can be trimmed to a shape that fits comfortably in the pot, with a 1–2 cm (½–¾ in) space all round the edges and underneath. If the fine roots are sparse, trim off about a third and fold the remainder underneath when replacing the tree in the pot.

6 Clean the pot with detergent, rinse it thoroughly and cover the drainage holes with mesh. Thread wire through the drainage holes for use later to hold the tree firm in the pot until the new roots have stabilized it. In large pots, you can add a drainage layer of coarse grit or gravel, but this isn't necessary with smaller pots. If your soil is sufficiently free-draining, a drainage layer shouldn't be necessary at all.

7 Place a layer of soil in the base of the pot, mounding it slightly where the trunk will sit – slightly off-centre looks best. This layer should be deep enough to allow room for new roots to grow, but not so deep that the base of the trunk is raised above the rim of the pot, which would make efficient watering very difficult. You may need several attempts before you get it right.

8 Place the tree in the pot with the base of the trunk on the mound of soil and settle it in by rotating the trunk back and forth a few times, while applying gentle downward pressure. Once you are satisfied with the position of the tree in the pot, draw the wires over the roots and twist them together – not too tightly – until the tree is held firm. These wires can be cut off in a couple of months, so leave the twisted ends where you can reach them.

9 Add more soil, working it between the roots with a sliver of wood or a pencil (or a chopstick, if you wish to be authentic). Be gentle and don't stab at the soil. Guide the stick between the roots and move it in a circular direction so that soil is worked into all the spaces between and under the roots as well as around the edges. Tap the sides of the pot with your fist from time to time to settle the soil.

10 Finally, bring the surface of the soil to a level just below the rim of the pot and water well. A good soaking is crucial at this stage to ensure that all the new soil is thoroughly wetted. Place the tree in a sheltered position, away from direct sun, cold draughts and frost, until the buds have begun to open. Don't feed for at least a month after repotting – allow the roots to recover their strength first.

Work fresh soil between the roots with a pointed stick. Make sure that all voids have been filled, especially underneath the outer roots.

Level off the soil, leaving the surface just below the rim of the pot, and water well. After watering, the soil may settle further, so you may need to add a little more to make up the level.

Selecting a pot

Normally, you would replant your bonsai in the same pot each time you prune the roots, but occasionally you may want to choose another one. Perhaps the tree has outgrown its original pot, or perhaps the colour or shape no longer suit the tree. The variety of shapes, sizes and colours is enormous, making the decision difficult. To a certain extent, the choice of pot depends on your personal taste, but there are a number of points to bear in mind which will make the decision easier.

Size and shape

A good bonsai pot will have generous drainage holes, a level base (to prevent pooling of water) and small feet to allow excess water to run away freely. It should not be glazed on the inside.

• In principle, slender trunks and group plantings look best in shallow pots, whereas thick trunks need deeper pots to maintain visual balance.

• Graceful, lowland styles of tree are set off best in oval pots or 'soft-cornered' rectangles with a curved profile. Bonsai with strong, angular or gnarled trunks need equally strong, rectangular-shaped pots.

• Wide, spreading styles look good in pots that flare outwards at the top or have a lip on the outer rim. Tall, slender trees are complemented by very simple, round pots.

• For the pot to be in correct visual proportion, it should be slightly narrower than the spread of the tree.

• Bonsai that cascade over the side of the container should be planted in special deep pots. Cascade pots are not only more suited to that style, but they are infinitely more practical. They are also more horticulturally sound in so far as they allow the root structure to echo that of the branches.

Colour

Bonsai pots are designed to complement the bonsai. Highly glazed, brightly coloured or heavily patterned pots will distract attention from the tree itself and destroy the harmony of the composition.

• Species with delicate foliage, such as Japanese maples or zelkovas, look good in pots with subdued pastel glazes. Elms, serissas, azaleas and dark-leaved deciduous trees can take a deeper colour.

LEFT These rare antique Chinese bonsai pots are a far cry from the more subdued designs and glazes that are popular today. However, their beauty makes them collector's items in their own right.

OPPOSITE Nests of more modestly priced modern bonsai pots.

ABOVE Bonsai pots are made in a bewildering variety of shapes, sizes and colours.

LEFT Rectangular pots with geometric details complement strong, heavy-trunked conifers or evergreen broad-leaved species.

These round 'drum' pots have a strong visual impact and suit tall, rugged pines.

• Junipers and yews, with their handsome chestnut-red bark, look good in subtle beige, brown or 'burnt-earth' colours with a matt, unglazed finish.

• The rich green needles and dark, craggy bark of pines are complemented by containers in rich browns or deep reds with interesting natural surface textures.

• To balance the extremely powerful effect of a flowering bonsai in full bloom, a more highly coloured pot is required. The choice of colour depends on your personal taste, but avoid really bright colours and high-gloss glazes. Consider the colour of the flowers and try to complement it. The exception to this general rule is in the case of azaleas, which are treated as non-flowering bonsai as far as the choice of pot is concerned.

Tall pots are specifically designed for cascade or semi-cascade styles.

Oval glazed pots suit zelkovas, maples and other deciduous species of graceful habit.

Fertilizers

All green plants require the three main plant nutrients – nitrogen, phosphorus and potassium. It is important that they get all these nutrients in order to thrive. An inadequate diet will cause symptoms such as general loss of vigour, poor flowering and reduced resistance to disease. A total absence of any one of these three will eventually cause the plant to die. They also need minute quantities of a number of trace elements such as magnesium, zinc, boron, molybdenum to name a few. Although required in only minute amounts, a deficiency of magnesium, for example, retards chlorophyll production resulting in the plant becoming weakened. Ensuring your trees get a balanced diet has been made easy by the wide range of commercial products currently available to the gardener, giving you plenty of choice.

Which type of fertilizer?

Fertilizers can be divided into two main types: organic and inorganic. Organic fertilizers are manufactured from plant or animal remains. Bone meal, dried blood, farmyard manure and garden compost all fall within this category. Inorganic fertilizers are manufactured from synthetic ingredients. As far as the three major nutrients are concerned, either type is capable of providing all that is necessary.

Both organic and inorganic fertilizers can be divided again into two groups: those intended for garden use and those intended for houseplants. Some houseplant fertilizers are intended to induce rapid, lush growth, which is undesirable on a bonsai. Avoid any that make this specific claim. Granular or dry garden fertilizers are intended for use on open ground, not in small containers, so judging the correct amount is impossible.

On the other hand, liquid garden fertilizers can be sprayed onto the foliage, which is a surprisingly efficient way of feeding plants, and doses can be judged precisely. The major drawbacks of foliar feeding are that it is impossible in wet weather and in dry weather foliar feeds tend to leave powdery deposits on the leaves.

The secret of success is to read the pack carefully before committing yourself, and to ensure that the contents include nutrients in the desired proportion (see page 56) and at least six trace elements. If there are no trace elements, you will have to apply a proprietary trace element supplement as well. Also check that the product is suitable for container-grown plants – either giving instructions for use as a foliar feed or stating application rates for a given volume of pot.

Bonsai fertilizers

These are basically no different from any other fertilizer, except that they are generally not so rich. They are formulated for all-round health and are ideal for general use.

The three major nutrients

On every pack of fertilizer, you should find reference to the NPK analysis. This tells you the strength and balance of the three major nutrients: nitrogen, phosphates and potash.

N – nitrogen
Nitrogen is responsible for promoting strong stems and healthy, dark leaves. Lack of nitrogen will result in thin, weak shoots and small, yellow leaves that rapidly fall. Too much nitrogen produces sappy stems and large leaves, both of which are vulnerable to fungal attack. Nitrogen is used up rapidly and so must be replenished regularly.

P – phosphates
Phosphates are necessary for strong, healthy roots and for prolific fruit production. A deficiency reduces root growth, causing general poor vigour and discoloured foliage. Flowering bonsai reluctant to set fruit should be given a high-phosphate fertilizer.

K – potash
Potash balances the effects of nitrogen. It is essential to flower production as well as to promoting resistance to fungal disease and generally hardening the plant against harsh environmental and climatic conditions. Scorched leaf margins – common on hornbeams and maples – may sometimes be avoided by increasing the potash content of the fertilizer. Increase the potash for flowering plants that are slow to bloom.

Following the letters 'NPK' will be three numbers such as: 'NPK 7:8:8'. These give the proportion of each ingredient and the strength of the fertilizer. For instance, NPK 7:8:8 contains seven parts of nitrogen, eight of phosphates and eight of potash. It is a well-balanced feed and is not too strong for bonsai. A product with NPK 25:15:15 is not only too high in nitrogen but also too rich for bonsai. Fertilizers with high NPK values should be diluted to half strength or even weaker.

Detailed advice on feeding particular species is given in the Tree Directory, pages 70–117.

Key

- Slow-release (3 months) granular fertilizer
- High-nitrogen (not for pines)
- Balanced fertilizer
- Low nitrogen: 0–10–10 if possible
- Rose or tomato fertilizer
- Slow-release for pines only

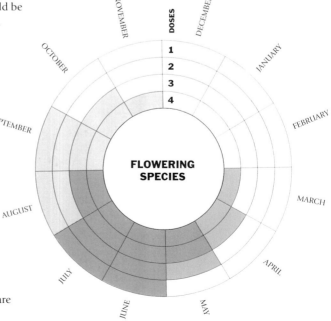

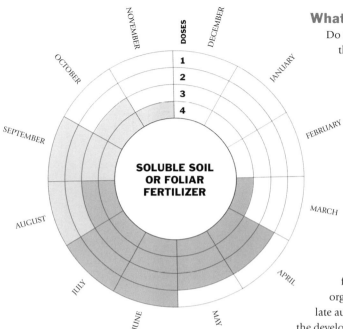

What to use when

Do not feed your trees more than they can use or when they don't need it, such as in autumn. Either could easily 'burn' the roots. Use general fertilizers at half strength, but apply twice as often as directed. The charts show the three basic feeding programmes, but there are some extra points to bear in mind. Most evergreens are slightly active during winter and will benefit from a low-strength, slow-release fertilizer such as bone meal or organic fertilizer pellets applied in late autumn. Broad-leaved species in the development stage will grow more vigorously with added nitrogen. Harden off the shoots with nitrogen-free feeds in late summer and autumn. High-nitrogen feeds applied in late summer will cause soft growth that will be killed off by the first hard frost, or will wilt over winter on indoor bonsai. They also retard flower bud production.

Increasing phosphate can aid the recovery of weak or recently repotted trees and encourages prolific fruiting on species such as cotoneaster, malus and pyracantha.

Nitrogen-free fertilizer, applied in late summer and early autumn, checks late growth, thickens trunks and branches and hardens the plant for winter. Increasing potash also encourages the thickening of trunks and branches as well as flowering.

Keeping in trim

All commercial bonsai are, to a certain extent, mass-produced, so no matter how much you pay, your bonsai will have imperfections that need to be rectified. There may be too many branches, or some may need repositioning. The younger twigs are sure to require attention – either now or in the near future. Also, the annual growth must be controlled in order to maintain your bonsai's perfect shape.

Pruning branches

Pruning branches on bonsai is a straightforward operation that requires just a little more care than pruning a garden shrub. With garden pruning, the wound heals rapidly as the trunk thickens, but on a bonsai, the process is slower. The healing tissues can form an unsightly swelling that would soon disappear on a full-size tree but will remain indefinitely on a bonsai. To avoid this, follow these simple steps.

Always prune in spring, when the tree is active and healing can begin at once. Autumn pruning may result in die-back of surrounding bark and summer pruning will cause unwanted shoots to grow from around the wound. First, cut the branch as close as you can to the trunk without damaging the bark on the trunk itself. Use sharp, 'by-pass' secateurs if you don't have special bonsai tools.

Using a wood-carver's gouge or strong modelling knife with a curved blade, begin to hollow out the wound. Work from the outside of the wound towards the centre, and keep your fingers out of the way in case the gouge slips! Inspect the wound from all angles periodically until you are satisfied that, from the side, the edge of the wound is flush with the trunk.

Continue hollowing until the cavity is about two or three annual rings deep. This ensures that, as the new, swollen healing tissue covers the wound, it 'rolls' into the cavity. By the time it has met in the centre of the wound, it will be flush with the surrounding bark.

The fresh wound must be sealed as soon as possible. Japanese cut paste is perfect for the job, but a home-made substitute will do just as well. Mix some red and green plasticine together until it more or less matches the colour of the bark, then add a little vegetable oil to prevent it rehardening. Press this evenly all over the wound, making certain that all the edges are well covered. As the wound heals, the plug of paste will be pushed off. Never use bitumen-based sealants or any other type that dries hard. These always stain the bark and can cause further damage when you try to remove them from the wound.

Regeneration pruning

If you have a branch that is too long, or has no side branches or only bears foliage at the very end, you can rectify this by shortening the branch in mid-summer. At this time of year, the tree's growth is in full flood and new shoots will spring from around the wound and, perhaps, further back along the remaining part of the branch. On branches that are less than 5 mm (¼ in) thick, it is advisable to prune to an internode or set of leaf scars which, on the majority of species, remains visible for several years. Conveniently, by the time the internodes disappear, the branch is mature enough to be pruned at any point with confidence. Seal the wound with cut paste as described above.

This technique is only suitable for deciduous species. On conifers, the offending branch should either be removed completely and a replacement wired into position from elsewhere, or you could try to introduce more curves in the branch to bring the side branches and foliage closer to the trunk.

Prune branches close to the trunk and carve away the stub, leaving a slightly hollow wound. Seal all wounds straight after pruning.

Pinching new growth

In order to maintain neat, clearly defined foliage pads, it is essential that the tree readily produces new buds on old wood so that the resulting shoots can be used to replace areas of foliage that have become overcrowded or have outgrown the design of the tree.

Deciduous trees

The new shoots that emerge in spring first bear two or three small leaves. As the shoot extends, each new leaf increases in size. To maintain small leaves and to keep the tree in shape, you must stop these new shoots extending before the leaves become too large.

You may need some tweezers for this job, unless you have nimble fingers. All you need to do is to wait until the shoot has two or three true leaves, then simply pinch out the tiny, soft tip. The shoot will grow no longer and the leaves will remain small. After a few weeks, another flush of smaller shoots will grow from latent buds as well as the buds in the axils of the remaining leaves.

If you allow the shoots to grow too long before pinching, you will then have to use scissors and cut back to two or three leaves. But beware: cutting back an older shoot can cause the next flush of growth to be too 'leggy', with large leaves.

If you want to extend a branch, let the shoot grow to the desired length, then cut it back by half. Repeat this process with the next flush of shoots, and so on, until you resort to tip pinching once again.

Junipers

Junipers either have scale-like foliage pressed tightly to the shoots, or sharp needles, generally borne in threes at each internode. To confuse the matter, junipers with scale-like foliage resort to needles following stress. This is known as juvenile foliage. All shoots bearing juvenile foliage should be pinched back in their first season, or cut out completely if there are only a few of them. If pinched in their second year, these shoots will wither and die without producing any new growth.

Pinching the normal shoots is done in one of two ways, depending on the nature of the shoot. Extension shoots are much plumper and generally paler in colour than the surrounding shoots. These should be cut back hard, right into last year's growth or even further. Cut back to a healthy pair of side shoots.

Once deciduous shoots have grown two full leaves, pinch out the soft growing tip.

To extend a branch, allow one shoot to grow until it begins to harden, before cutting it back.

Cut the shoot back to the point where you want the first fork to come.

To keep the foliage clouds neat, the tip of all other shoots must be broken off. (Using scissors for this job will make the cut tips turn brown.) Grasp a fan of foliage between the thumb and finger of one hand and pull away the tips with the other. Rolling the tips as you pull helps them to break cleanly. This process is quite time-consuming and should be repeated several times during the growing season, which can continue long after deciduous trees have adopted their autumn colour.

Flowering bonsai

If you pinch out the tips of flowering bonsai in the same way as other deciduous species, you will prevent the formation of next year's flower buds. With the exception of azaleas and some tropicals, the flower buds are formed at the base of the previous season's shoots.

To maximize next year's blossoms, trim your bonsai to shape immediately after flowering and allow all new growth to grow unchecked until mid- to late summer. Once the shoots have stopped extending, examine the buds at the base carefully. You should be able to see that they are rounder or larger than those further along the shoot. These are the flower buds. Cut the shoots back, leaving two or three of these buds.

Next year, the new shoots that are produced from the base of the flowers will be short – perhaps only bearing two or three leaves. These are the beginnings of flowering spurs that do not extend but continue to bear flowers year after year, until they eventually become so crowded that they need to be thinned out.

Azaleas

Azaleas are valued not only for their flowers but also for their neat foliage and strong trunks and branches. Commercial azaleas are invariably varieties of Japanese satsuki azalea, whose flower buds are produced at the tips of last year's shoots and open after this year's have already begun to grow.

On junipers, a few shoots will appear fatter and grow more rapidly than others. These should be cut back hard, leaving just one or two side shoots.

To pinch the remaining foliage, grasp tufts of shoots between finger and thumb, and pull off the tips.

Immediately after flowering, cut back into last year's growth, removing the spent flower head and any new growth that emerged at its base. Ideally, you should allow a few of last year's leaves to remain. It is a good idea at this stage to thin out last year's shoots, leaving only two at each fork. This prevents overcrowding and encourages new buds to form on old wood, from which replacement branches can be built in the future.

Any over-vigorous extension shoots should be cut back to the base.

Pines

Pines have a unique growth pattern. In the wild, most pines rarely throw out new growth from old branches, and only do so in response to damage or stress. Here lies the answer. Bonsai growers developed a pruning technique that, by utilizing and controlling the tree's response mechanism, enables them to encourage pines to produce buds where they are needed with a fair degree of predictability. The secret is in the timing.

First stage: In spring, pine buds don't actually open to allow the embryonic shoot to emerge. Instead, they gradually elongate, tearing the fragile, papery sheath that protects them. (These elongating shoots are called 'candles', for fairly obvious reasons.) As the sheath disintegrates, you will see tiny, bright green 'scales', which are the developing needles. We will call this the first stage.

Second stage: By the time the candles reach about half of their eventual length, the groups of needles, about 2–5 mm ($\frac{1}{16}$–$\frac{1}{4}$ in) long, start to peel away slowly. When they stand at about a 20-degree angle to the candle, they begin to separate into individual needles, still bright, fresh green. This is the second stage.

Third stage: The candles elongate further and the needles lengthen and separate entirely from each other, darkening in colour as they do so. The semi-mature needles are almost as dark as last year's, but only half the length of full-grown needles, and are still shiny and slender. This is the third stage.

Fourth stage: Finally, if left untouched, by mid-summer the shoots are fully mature. The needles have darkened and lost some of their sheen, and now stand well away from the shoot. The shoot itself has lost its juvenile green colour and has turned a pale brown or grey colour – the fourth stage.

Cause and effect

By timing the pinching out of all or part of the candles, you can achieve different results, but there are a few points to bear in mind before you begin.

Always start with the lowest, therefore the weakest, branch, and do the smallest candles first. This process guarantees that they will get a fair share of the healing auxins (hormones) before the more vigorous candles are pruned.

Do all the small candles on the tree first, spreading the work over a week or so. Then

After stress, junipers produce uncharacteristic juvenile foliage. Isolated juvenile shoots can be cut out. Larger areas should be lightly pinched, and the shoots removed only when sufficient adult foliage has developed to replace them.

Spring-flowering deciduous species, such as crab apples and cherries, must be allowed to grow unchecked until the end of the summer, when they should be cut back to leave only the flower buds at the base.

return to the stronger candles on the lowest branch and so on. Vary the amount you break off according to the comparative size of the candle. Break about one-third off the small candles and at least two-thirds off the very largest candles. You can increase this if you wait until the third stage before beginning pruning. Where there are clusters of shoots in close proximity, remove some of them entirely, leaving no more than two shoots emerging from the same point.

If you begin candle pruning as the first stage of growth reaches completion, two or three buds will form at the wound during the summer, and perhaps at the base of the shoot. They will be large and vigorous, and will grow strongly next year.

By the time you have finished this process, the larger candles will be almost at the end of the second stage. Pruning shoots at this time will help promote new buds on last year's growth – ideal for replacing the over-vigorous shoot you have just pruned.

Pruning towards the end of the third stage will reduce the vigour of the shoot and will result in a larger number of much smaller buds at its base and on last year's growth, possibly on two-year-old wood as well. There will be extremely few, if any, buds produced at the wound.

By late summer, the shoot is fully mature and next year's buds have begun to develop. At this time, you can remove the shoot completely, leaving only a short stub (provided there are sufficient old needles remaining to nourish the branch). In healthy trees, this will result in a mass of tiny buds forming during the winter months on wood several years old. These new buds are extremely delicate and difficult to spot, and will need two seasons' growth before they are strong enough to be trained as replacement branches.

Needle pulling

Old needles should be removed periodically by pulling them out one by one. This allows light and air into the tree and makes new bud production more prolific. It also allows you to assess the branch structure and to apply wire if necessary. Remove more needles from the top of the tree than from the lower branches, thereby countering the tree's natural tendency to concentrate its energy in the apex. Autumn or early spring are the best times for this.

As pine buds extend in late spring, they must be pinched back by bending them until they snap cleanly.

A strict regime of pinching and needle pulling will encourage the formation of adventitious buds on older parts of the branches. These are essential to build up density of foliage and to replace overgrown areas in the future.

Shaping with wire

The principle behind wire training bonsai is simple. If a piece of wire of an appropriate thickness is coiled around a branch, the two together can be bent and the wire will hold the branch in position. As the branch grows, it thickens as new wood is produced. This new wood conforms to the new shape of the branch. In addition, the pressure of the wire on the bark increases as the branch thickens, and the wood beneath it becomes compressed and much more dense. The combination of these two factors means that, after a suitable period, the wire can be removed and the branch will remain in place.

The length of time it takes for a branch to set depends on the species, the season and the thickness of the branch. More detailed information is given in the Tree Directory, pages 70–117, but as a general principle, young deciduous shoots and twigs can set within a matter of a month or so, while springy conifer branches can take several years.

Once positioned, check the branches regularly, especially at the top of the tree where the growth is strongest. As soon as the wire appears to be biting into the bark, remove it immediately before it causes ugly scars. If the branch has not set satisfactorily, rewire it, coiling the wire in the opposite direction to minimize the damage to the bark.

Always cut off the wire with sharp wire cutters that are able to cut right to the tip of the jaws. It may seem easier and certainly more economical to uncoil the wire, but this often tears the bark, and is certainly a false economy in the long run.

Which wire?

In Japan, annealed (softened) copper wire is invariably used for all conifers because of its greater holding power and aluminium wire for deciduous trees. In the West, aluminium wire is used for all species by most enthusiasts simply because it is much cheaper, even when used double on heavier branches. Special brown, anodized aluminium wire is stocked in many sizes by all bonsai suppliers.

However, if you have access to offcuts of electrical cable, you can salvage copper wire in a variety of sizes. This can be annealed by heating it in a bonfire until it is red hot and then quickly submerging it in cold water for a couple of seconds. The action of coiling it around the branch, then bending the branch

1 Coil the wire at a 45-degree angle, in contact with the bark but not so tight as to bruise it.

2 On long branches or trunks, the wire used for the base may be too thick to use further along. You can transfer to thinner wire at a convenient point, overlapping the two by several turns to ensure good anchorage.

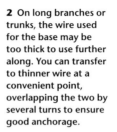

3 When wiring a single branch, anchor the wire firmly by coiling it around the trunk several times.

4 Better still, use one piece of wire for two nearby branches. Make sure that the wire goes through each branch 'fork' in the same direction, as shown.

5 Use one piece of wire to shape both arms of a 'fork', like this. Again, make sure both ends of the wire pass through the fork in the same direction.

6 Here, two parallel wires have been used to shape the thick part of the branch. Then one is diverted to shape a side branch, while the other continues along the main branch.

and wire together, hardens the wire, resulting in more than doubling its strength.

Plastic-coated iron wire, sold in garden nurseries for tying up climbers and so on, is too rigid for bonsai use. Also, as it is coiled around the branch, the plastic coating tends to rupture, causing the core to rust, which then stains or even corrodes the bark.

How to wire

Before you begin, practise on a twig cut from a garden shrub until you have gained a little confidence. Then test the branch you are about to wire for its resistance and try to find the thickness of wire that is slightly stiffer. You will find that it takes only a short while to become quite expert at gauging the right thickness of wire for any given branch. Cut a piece of wire that is at least one-and-a-half times as long as

7 When bending wired branches, use your thumbs as a fulcrum. Try not to make too sharp a bend at first.

8 Once the branch has set, or when the wire has become too tight, it should be cut off. Never try to unwind the wire as you will risk damaging the bark.

9 Leaving the wire on the branch for too long will cause scars that will take many years to heal – if ever. It may even become completely buried. These scars were made eight years ago and still have a long way to go.

the branch. If the wire is to hold the branch securely, it must first of all be firmly anchored. Do this by coiling it a couple of turns around the trunk or alternatively around the parent branch if you are wiring secondary growth. Begin coiling the wire around the branch at an angle of about 45 degrees. Hold each turn of the wire with one hand while you coil the next, in order to avoid exerting too much pressure on the bark.

Bend the branch by using your thumbs as fulcrums on the inside of the curve and spreading the pressure of your fingers along as much of the branch as possible. Bend in stages, listening carefully for cracking bark, at which point stop! If the branch has still not achieved the desired position, return to it every two or three weeks and bend it a little further until you are satisfied.

The intricate grain of exposed heartwood, bleached and preserved, can add character and a sense of mystery to an otherwIse mundane tree.

Deadwood on bonsai

In nature, many old conifers, especially those growing in mountainous regions, display areas of deadwood that have become bleached by the sun and contrast dramatically with the colours of the bark and foliage. Caused by storms, drought or natural die-back, the deadwood tells us about the harsh conditions that the tree has had to endure.

Japanese masterpiece junipers and pines, which have been developed from plants collected from the mountains, invariably have large areas of deadwood and are consequently highly prized. The deadwood is further refined or extended by the artist using a variety of carving techniques until, in some cases, an almost abstract design is achieved.

Commercial conifer bonsai, particularly junipers, have artificially created deadwood areas, either whole branches (in bonsai terms these are called *jins*) or on parts of the trunk (termed *sharis*). These relieve the visual monotony and also greatly enhance the bonsai's dynamic image.

Jins and sharis

Creating your own jins and sharis is quite a simple process, but should only be done after careful consideration. Too much deadwood clumsily handled will detract from the overall appearance of the bonsai and will be impossible to rectify. Jins and sharis can be made at almost any time of year, provided that the tree can be kept in frost-free conditions until the wounds have healed. But the best time is in late summer, when the sap is not rising so quickly and the wounds are less likely to 'bleed'. Also, the wounds still have time to heal before winter and the exposed heartwood will dry out within a few weeks.

Jins

Once you have decided which branch to convert to a jin, shorten it to about 2 cm (¾ in) longer than the eventual desired length of the jin. Then, with a sharp modelling knife, cut through the bark around the base of the branch. Cut right through to the heartwood, making a vertical 'eye' shape. This will look more natural when it has healed and is less likely to interrupt the flow of sap past the jin. If you do this in spring or summer, the bark on the branch will come away remarkably easily. Squeeze the branch gently with pliers to separate it from the heartwood and just pull it off. If you try to create jins in autumn or winter, you will have to scrape the bark away with a knife, because by this time it will have become fused to the heartwood.

The easiest way to create a natural effect is to peel away the surface layers of heartwood to expose the inner grain. Do this by crushing the end of the jin with the pliers and carefully pulling back small sections of wood until the desired effect is achieved. As you near the base of the jin, be careful not to pull too hard or you may find that you have pulled away part of the wood beneath the bark on the trunk as well.

Jagged splinters and fluffy grain can be removed by burning them off with a candle flame or similar. The heat from the flame will also soften the resin in the jin, enabling you to bend it to a new position, which it will retain once the resin has cooled. This technique can be effective on jins up to two or three years old!

Finally, the jin must be preserved and bleached to imitate the effect found in nature. This is done with the periodic application of lime-sulphur compound, which penetrates the wood and acts as a fungicide. The foul-smelling liquid is yellow when applied, but as it dries it turns silvery white. Some brands dry too white and should be mixed with a small amount of black ink to tone down the colour.

MAKING A JIN

1 To make a jin, first cut through the bark around the base of the branch stub, then cut along its length. The bark should peel away quite easily.

2 Next, crush the end of the stub with pliers and peel away strips of wood to expose the inner grain.

3 When finished, the jin should appear natural, as if the branch had broken in a storm many years ago.

Sharis

Sharis are best created in mid- to late summer when the bark will peel away easily. However, before you start to create a shari, you must first consider two very important points: will the removal of bark from the chosen part of the trunk retard the growth of any branches immediately above it, and will the shari appear natural?

To ensure that the shari will not interrupt the sap flow to upper branches, examine the bark closely. You should see faint swellings in the bark, running vertically. These indicate the main sap flow lines from root to branch and, provided these are left more or less intact, there should be no problem. Junipers and pines both have the ability to transfer sap sideways to a certain extent, so you can be a little daring here.

For the shari to appear natural, it should follow roughly the same line as the trunk. For example, if the trunk spirals to the left, make the shari do likewise; exaggerating the curves a little will make the shari more dynamic. Making the shari spiral in the opposite direction will not only look incongruous but will also risk interrupting the sap flow.

If possible, incorporate some existing or new jins in the shari for added interest and realism. Always ensure that some living bark is clearly visible on all parts of the trunk – ideally, no less than 30 per cent of the width of the trunk should consist of living bark.

First, mark the edges of the proposed shari with a water-based ink. (If you change your mind, it will easily wash off.) Consider the lines carefully before you begin to work. Cut through the bark with a sharp modelling knife, taking care not to let it slip. It is important to cut right through the bark at the first attempt. Make a second cut about 2 mm (¹⁄₁₆ in) inside the first, angling the knife so that the two cuts meet at the heartwood. The thin sliver of bark between the two cuts will pull away easily, enabling you to insert another blade under the main part of the bark to be removed. This should come away in one piece. Seal the exposed edges of the bark with cut paste to retain moisture and treat the exposed wood with lime-sulphur solution. Wetting the wood with a fine spray helps it to absorb the solution.

Once the exposed heartwood has dried, you can add interest by carving or routing to emphasize the grain. Try scraping the wood with a hard wire brush for a pleasing texture.

MAKING A SHARI

1 First, mark out the area of bark to be stripped. Make sure that the shari follows the natural line of the trunk.

2 The effect of stripping the bark from one side of the trunk, incorporating several jins, is dramatic.

3 Once finished, the shari and jins should be treated with lime sulphur to preserve and bleach the wood. Lime sulphur smells strongly of rotten eggs, so do this outside! The yellow solution fades to white as it dries.

Maintenance

Jins and sharis require very little routine maintenance apart from an annual clean with a wire brush and the occasional application of lime sulphur. However, every few years you will need to take your modelling knife and redefine the jins and sharis by cutting the bark back to its original position or beyond.

SYMBOLS

Hardiness

tender

half-hardy

tolerates light frost

tolerates heavy freezing

Difficulty

easy

needs special care

difficult

Sun/Shade

full sun

semi-shade

shade

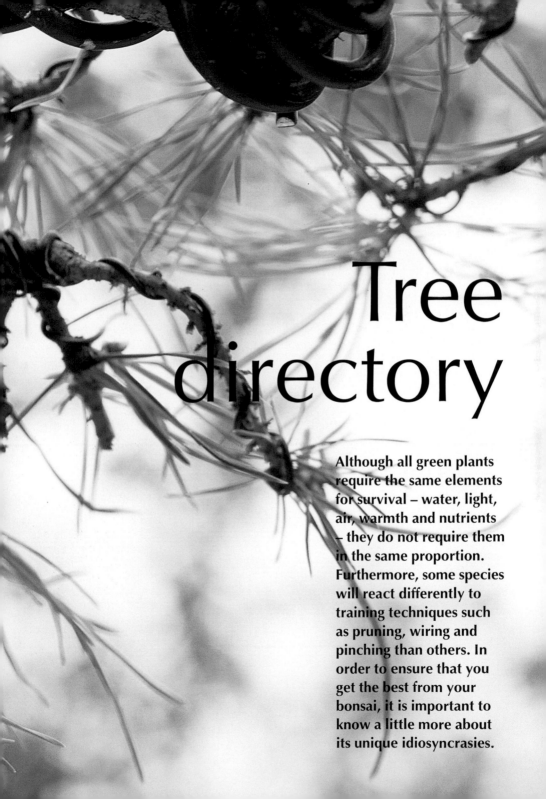

Tree directory

Although all green plants require the same elements for survival – water, light, air, warmth and nutrients – they do not require them in the same proportion. Furthermore, some species will react differently to training techniques such as pruning, wiring and pinching than others. In order to ensure that you get the best from your bonsai, it is important to know a little more about its unique idiosyncrasies.

Acer buergerianum
Trident Maple

Outdoor

Trident maples are common parkland and street trees throughout the Far East and are popular for their rapid growth and brilliant autumn colour. The bark on older trees becomes grey and cracked, but when confined to a container it remains pale grey with a pink flush, complementing the mid-green foliage.

In Japan, where almost all commercial trident maples are grown, the species' rapid growth and thick, fleshy roots are exploited to produce a wide variety of styles. In recent years, the fashion has been for thick, tapering trunks with strong buttresses where the roots flare at the base. These are produced in the thousands for export – a trunk 6 cm (2¼ in) thick being achieved in five or six years. Forest or group plantings are also common, comprising young plants of varying heights and thicknesses.

Trident maples are the kings of the root-over-rock style of bonsai. The tree is planted over a jagged rock, representing a mountainside or cliff face, and its roots clasp the rock tightly until they finally plunge into the soil. As the roots thicken with age, a process that is hastened by the sun-warmed rocks, they become welded together where they touch and create the illusion of great age and strength.

Where to keep trident maple

Trident maples should be kept outdoors at all times except during periods of heavy frost, when they will need to be brought into a frost-free shed. They can be displayed indoors for a few days at a time while they are in leaf.

Trident maples enjoy full sun so long as the roots are not allowed to become too dry, in which case the margins of the leaves will burn. It is best to provide some afternoon shade. Protect from strong winds at all times.

Trident maples are often planted with their thick roots clinging tightly to a rock, creating really dramatic images.

Maintenance

Repotting Every one to three years in early spring. Trident maples are the first deciduous trees to come into leaf, especially if kept frost-free all winter. Thick roots can be hard pruned, almost up to the trunk. Use Akadama or the standard bonsai soil mix.

Pruning Very early spring, two weeks before repotting. Pruning branches in mid-summer induces prolific adventitious growth.

Pinching Pinch out the tips of all new shoots when two complete leaves have formed. Repeat as necessary throughout the year.

Watering Trident maples dislike any hint of dryness in the soil. Drench the soil each morning in summer and check the soil again late afternoon, watering if dry just below the surface. Keep soil moist but not wet in winter.

Feeding Balanced feed from bud-burst until late summer, then low- or zero-nitrogen feed.

Beware! When the thick roots on trident maples are allowed to freeze solid, they can literally burst. Preventing the soil from becoming too wet in winter helps considerably, but protection from hard frosts is mandatory.

Acer palmatum
Japanese Maple

Outdoor

Japanese maples are among the most beautiful trees on earth. Their slender, arching branches support an open canopy of delicate, lobed leaves, whose subtle colours intensify to reds and oranges in autumn. They are very graceful, elegant trees, and this is echoed in bonsai.

These maples are notoriously variable when grown from seed, which means that there are countless different strains available for bonsai. The leaves vary in spring from bronze, through orange to bright red, turning to various shades of green in summer, often with red margins.

The shoots – often coloured red or orange – are fine, and grow prolifically from internodes on old wood or from around pruning wounds. These clusters must be thinned out, leaving a maximum of two at any one point. Failure to do this will result in swollen knotty structures that will spoil the elegance of your bonsai.

Large-scale production of commercial trees leads to a number of poor-quality examples in each shipment. Uneven roots or ugly pruning scars are not uncommon, so choose carefully.

Where to keep Japanese maple

They should be kept outdoors at all times except during periods of heavy frost, when they should be brought into a frost-free outhouse. They can be displayed indoors for a few days while in leaf or for an hour or so in winter. Japanese maples will tolerate full sun so long as the roots are not allowed to become too dry and they are not exposed to strong winds.

Japanese maples are graceful, elegant trees with delicate leaves. This specimen *Acer palmatum* is planted in a pot created by British ceramic artist Gordon Duffett.

Maintenance

Repotting Every one to three years in spring, as the buds begin to elongate and adopt a sheen. Use Akadama or the standard soil mix. Add some sphagnum moss in hard-water areas.

Pruning In spring, two weeks before repotting. Pruning branches in mid-summer results in masses of new shoots from the internodes.

Pinching Pinch out the tips of all new shoots when two or four complete leaves have formed. Repeat as necessary throughout the year.

Watering Use rainwater instead of tap water if possible, as they need slightly acidic soil conditions. Keep soil moist at all times, avoiding both waterlogging and dryness. Spray foliage regularly.

Feeding Balanced feed from bud-burst until late summer, followed by low- or zero-nitrogen feed. Apply a soil acidifier twice a year in hard-water areas.

Beware! Aphids colonize young shoots in spring and distort the new leaves. In winter, a cold wind can kill fine shoots; in summer, leaves can become scorched by little more than a gentle breeze, so wind protection is essential.

Acer palmatum 'Chishio'/'Deshôjô' Japanese Red Maple

Outdoor

The leaves of red maples emerge bright scarlet in spring and return to that colour in autumn. If kept in bright but not sunny conditions, the leaves can remain red all summer, but in most years they will display a range of leaf colours. Cutting off all leaves in mid-summer induces a fresh crop of red leaves, smaller than the first. These stand a better chance of remaining undamaged by autumn and produce a better display, but this should only be done on strong trees and then only in alternate years.

Red maples are rather slow-growing – more so in containers – so when buying, it is best to spend a little extra for a more developed tree.

Where to keep Japanese red maple

Keep outdoors except when temperatures dip much below freezing for more than a few days, when they should be taken into a frost-free shed. They can be displayed indoors for a few days at a time while they are in leaf or for an hour or so in winter. Even a few days indoors in spring can turn the red leaves to dull green.

They are easily scorched by sun or wind, so must be protected. Provide shade from the afternoon sun yet adequate light by placing in the shadow of a nearby tree or building.

Maintenance

Repotting Every one to three years in spring, as the buds begin to elongate and shine. Keep absolutely frost-free after repotting. Use Akadama or the standard soil mix.

Pruning In spring, two weeks before or after repotting. Thin out overcrowded branches and twigs. Prune out old knots and spurs by cutting

True red maples are less vigorous than most other varieties and need extra protection from wind. The red spring colour often fades towards green in summer but returns in the autumn.

back to a shoot or bud that can be allowed to grow on as a replacement.

Pinching Pinch out the tips of all new shoots when two or four complete leaves have formed. Repeat as necessary throughout the year. Leave late-summer growth unchecked to build up vigour before a final trim in early autumn.

Watering Use rainwater instead of tap water. Keep soil moist at all times; avoid waterlogging and dryness. Spray foliage regularly.

Feeding Balanced feed from bud-burst until late summer, then low- or zero-nitrogen feed. Use soil acidifier twice yearly in hard-water areas.

Beware! Spray monthly against aphids. When protecting from wind, ensure good ventilation to all parts of the tree to avoid powdery mildew.

Acer palmatum 'Kiyohime'
Kiyohime Maple

Outdoor

Kiyohime maple bonsai are quite rare and consequently more expensive than other varieties of maple, due to their extremely slow rate of growth and tendency to grow into a low, spreading shrub – both of which make bonsai culture difficult. Once the bonsai image has been achieved, maintaining it requires a little more careful consideration and attention to detail than other maples. However, the trouble taken is worthwhile because the tiny, bright green leaves and dense tracery of fine twigs can form a convincing image of a full-grown tree, even on very small bonsai.

Kiyohime are invariably grown as a broom-style bonsai, where all the branches emanate from more or less the same point at the top of a straight trunk and fan out in all directions. Kiyohime look especially good in winter, when their fine twig structure is clearly visible.

Where to keep kiyohime maple

Keep outdoors at all times. Although technically hardy, kiyohime growing in containers should be regarded as half-hardy and so taken into a frost-free building when temperatures dip much below freezing. They can be displayed indoors for a few days while they are in leaf or for an hour or so in winter.

Kiyohime maples are very easily scorched by sun or wind. Shadow cast by a house or fence is better than overhead shading; if overhead shade is too dense, the inherently weak apex on kiyohime may lose vigour and die back.

Maintenance

Repotting Every one to three years in spring, as the buds begin to elongate and show green between the scales. Keep absolutely frost-free after repotting. Use Akadama or the standard soil mix. Add some sphagnum moss in hard-water areas to increase acidity.

Pruning In spring, two weeks before or after repotting. Thin out overcrowded branches and twigs. Never hard prune the leader or the upward-growing branches that form the apex. Kiyohime have a natural horizontal habit and are reluctant to regenerate a wounded apex.

Pinching Pinch out the tips of all new shoots when two or four leaves have formed. Repeat as necessary throughout the year. Allow the apex to gain vigour before cutting back to two leaves.

Watering Use rainwater instead of tap water if possible, as they need slightly acidic soil. Keep soil moist at all times, avoiding waterlogging and dryness. Spray foliage regularly.

Feeding Balanced feed from bud-burst until late summer, then low- or zero-nitrogen feed. Use soil acidifier twice yearly in hard-water areas.

Beware! Avoid all unnecessary damage to the branches that form the apex, as that part of the tree is weakest and lacks the vigour to recover.

Kiyohime maples are naturally low, spreading shrubs and are ideally suited to this particular style of bonsai.

Arundinaria
Bamboo

Indoor

In recent years, varieties of bamboo have become increasingly popular as subjects for indoor bonsai because of their typically Oriental appearance, but they are seldom used by serious collectors in either China or Japan. Specimen bamboo bonsai are rare and are always planted in large groupings on stone slabs or in large shallow trays, imitating the dense groves familiar in Far-Eastern countries.

Bamboos are grasses and, therefore, do not form branches so cannot be trained into tree forms. Instead, new shoots emerge from below soil level to add to the grove and are pinched out at the desired height. During the next few years, the stems thicken and the tufts of foliage become more abundant until, eventually, the stem becomes too bushy and has to be cut out at the base and replaced by a younger one.

If any one stem is allowed to become disproportionately large, it will dominate the others. Bearing in mind that all the stems are growing from the same interconnected root system, dominant stems will take more than their fair share of water and nutrients until the smaller and weaker stems wither and die. This natural process is not so desirable in bonsai.

Where to keep bamboo

Most varieties of bamboo are more or less hardy when grown in the ground, but in containers they are less tolerant of cold. Ideally, all bamboo should spend their summers outside, but they are content to stay indoors all year if they receive enough light and fresh air.

Keep close to a sunny window but where the bonsai will be shaded from direct sun during the hottest part of the day. Outdoors, bamboo can receive as much sun as you like, provided the soil is not allowed to dry out.

Maintenance

Repotting Every two to three years in spring or autumn. Cut 'wedges' out of the dense root system and discard or replant elsewhere. The remaining sections can be rearranged in the pot to improve the design. Place the thickest stems towards the centre and the smaller ones towards the rear and sides, creating the illusion of perspective. Use the standard soil mix with a couple of extra handfuls of organic matter. If planting on a slab or rock, make sure that there are no hollows in the surface to trap water.

Pruning Cut out overgrown or dominant stems just below soil level with a sharp knife. Unwanted new shoots can be plucked out when still young and soft.

Pinching When each stem has achieved the desired height, pluck out the growing tip with tweezers. Thin out side growth to maintain a natural bamboo-like appearance.

Watering Bamboo love moist soil but suffer from severe root rot in waterlogged conditions. Use a free-draining container and water frequently during hot weather – three or four times a day. If this is not possible, use a deeper container that will require less frequent watering but will not be so aesthetically harmonious with the stems and foliage.

Feeding Half-strength balanced fertilizer during the growing season with a low-nitrogen top-up in autumn. A weak balanced feed in winter will keep bamboo grown in warm homes in good condition.

Beware! Waterlogged soil will kill bamboo as quickly as drought.

The supple stems of bamboo sway gracefully in the gentlest of breezes, evoking the fundamental atmosphere of the Orient.

Bougainvillea
Bougainvillea

Indoor & Outdoor

Originally from South America, these semi-evergreen climbers are nowadays a familiar sight in gardens throughout the Mediterranean region. Their colourful bracts, often mistaken for flowers, vary from white, through all shades of pink to rich crimson, and are borne in late summer to early autumn. The tiny flowers are nestled in the centres of these bracts.

To produce a large bonsai, the plant has to be grown in open ground for many years until a thick trunk base develops, whereupon all growth is removed and the new branch structure can be grown and trained.

Where to keep bougainvillea

They adore full sun throughout the summer, indoors or out. Outdoors, it is less easy to control the water, and flowering may be inconsistent. Indoors, hot sun through window glass is intensified, so some light shade such as an open-weave net curtain is beneficial in the hottest part of the day. Keep on the cool side – 8–15°C (46–59°F) – in winter. If all the leaves fall, the plant is in a draught or has become too cold or been overwatered. Move to a better position and moderate watering.

Maintenance

Repotting Every three to five years in spring, removing all the old, spent soil. Don't be too severe with pruning the roots. Use a deeper than normal pot and increase the organic content to 80 per cent, keeping it coarse and well aerated.

Pruning Branch pruning can be carried out at any time while the plant is semi-dormant. Prune current season's growth hard straight after flowering. Leave spring growth unchecked until the first few leaves have hardened, when

ABOVE Unlike many climbers, bougainvillea will readily produce a fine branch structure.

LEFT The richly coloured bracts – often mistaken for petals – are the main point of interest in exotic bougainvillea bonsai.

they are cut back to one or two leaves. The following flush of growth will bear the flowers. Pruning too early will induce too much vegetative growth; too late will retard flowering.

Watering The soil surface can be bone dry in winter, but the colour should darken slightly with moisture beneath. When buds begin to swell in spring, give a thorough watering and then keep moist but never saturated.

Feeding Low-nitrogen feed, such as rose or tomato fertilizer. While growing, only feed monthly.

Beware! Moving your bougainvillea from one environment to another without gradual acclimatization can cause defoliation and retard flowering. Always introduce it to its new quarters in stages over a two-week period.

Carmona microphylla
Fukien Tea

Indoor

Some people find Fukien tea very hard to look after, but it can be an ideal species for indoor bonsai. This common Asiatic garden shrub will thrive in hot, steamy kitchens and on sunny windowsills that do not cool down at night.

The small, neat leaves are a rich, glossy green and are borne on stout shoots that spring out from all parts of the tree. The shoots are so prolific that you can reshape the tree in a very short time simply by trimming it like a topiary hedge. Periodically, the older foliage-bearing spurs must be thinned out to prevent inner growth dying from lack of light and air. This is an ideal opportunity to refine the branch structure and make a more tree-like framework to support the new foliage. Try to introduce spaces between different layers of foliage to make the tree look older and more dignified.

Flowering is induced by heat and humidity, so if you can maintain both at a high level, you will have masses of small, white flowers all year round. For best results, the temperature should not fall below 20°C (68°F), even at night. Stand the pot in a tray of water, supported on stones so that the drainage holes are clear of the water, to increase local humidity.

Where to keep fukien tea

Carmonas adore sunshine and perform poorly in shady conditions. After acclimatization, your carmona can stay in full sun outside all summer, but should be brought into a sunny window as soon as the nights become cooler. If kept indoors all summer, check that the afternoon sun through the glass is not burning the foliage and reposition the tree if necessary. Avoid moving it around too much as carmonas dislike excessive fluctuations in temperature.

Maintenance

Repotting Every two to three years in spring, using a little extra coarse organic matter. Water sparingly for a week afterwards to encourage the new roots to grow in search of moisture.

Pruning Branches can be pruned at any time. Thin out congested areas to allow more light and air to penetrate and to induce fresh growth.

Pinching Pinch out shoots that threaten to spoil the outline of the tree as the need arises.

Watering Keep the soil well moistened in winter and water prolifically in summer. Spray the foliage regularly to improve flowering. Plunge the pot in a bowl of water periodically.

Feeding Low-nitrogen feed whenever the tree is in active growth. Stop feeding if growth ceases for a while in cool rooms during winter.

Beware! Only a hint of frost or icy draught can be fatal. Treat for aphid infestations with insecticides recommended for indoor plants.

Carmonas can be difficult to maintain, but they make an ideal species for indoor bonsai. This one is just about to come into flower.

Carpinus
Hornbeam

Outdoor

The two varieties of hornbeam most commonly used for bonsai production are *Carpinus laxiflora*, Japanese hornbeam, and *C. turczaninowii*, Korean hornbeam. All hornbeams have neat, oval leaves with finely toothed margins and depressed veins. The Japanese hornbeam has pale grey bark that develops wavy streaks of paler grey running from roots to apex as it matures. The Korean hornbeam has a darker grey bark with mahogany hints. Very few species can equal its rich orange autumn colour.

The twigs and branches are deceptively supple but can crack when bent too far. Bend each branch a little at first, then at weekly intervals, until you achieve the final position.

Where to keep hornbeam

Hornbeams are theoretically tolerant of full sun, but in hot weather the roots seem unable to draw water as quickly as it evaporates from the leaves. The result is scorching of the leaf margins. Position away from any direct sun after late morning. In winter, the tree can be left outside provided the temperature is not below -7°C (19°F). If colder, take into a shed or garage, but don't leave for more than an hour above 5°C (41°F) or it might break dormancy.

Maintenance

Repotting Every two years in spring, as buds begin to swell. Use Akadama or standard soil mix. (Provide extra shade and be extra-vigilant with watering if using Akadama.)

Pruning Branches can be pruned at any time between leaf-fall and spring. Thin out congested areas and shorten overextended growth in mid-summer.

Pinching Pinch out tips of new shoots when two true leaves have formed.

Watering Water copiously when in growth. Never allow the soil to become even slightly dry. In winter, maintain soil evenly moist.

Feeding Balanced feed from spring to late summer, followed by low-nitrogen or nitrogen-free feed in autumn. Overfeeding can cause weak growth extra-prone to scorch in the sun.

Beware! Hot sun and drying winds can have a devastating effect on the leaves of a hornbeam grown in a shallow container.

The grey striped bark of Japanese hornbeam creates the illusion of an old tree, and is especially effective in forest plantings.

Celtis sinensis
Chinese Hackberry

Outdoor

Chinese hackberry is a deciduous tree with small oval leaves and fine twigs. The leaves and internodes (spaces between leaves on the shoot) reduce well in response to constant trimming and pinching, and back-budding is prolific, making this an ideal species for bonsai. The flowers, which appear in spring, are small and insignificant, but the bright orange fruit are extremely attractive and unique among deciduous bonsai species. However, the fruit are reluctant to set in temperate climates, so special treatment is needed to encourage better performance. Spray several times a day from spring onwards and place the tree over or close to a tray of water to maintain high local humidity. On cool evenings, bring into the kitchen to maintain temperature and humidity.

Where to keep hackberry

Although fully hardy, the fact that most celtis bonsai originate in China and Taiwan means that they are generally imported by dealers in indoor bonsai and are often sold as such. They can survive well indoors all year round but must be kept below 8°C (46°F) during the winter to ensure that the tree has a sufficient dormant period. Place on a balcony or outside windowsill sheltered from the wind. During summer, your celtis will need to be close to an open sunny window. Poor light and ventilation will result in weak, leggy growth and persistent attacks of powdery mildew.

Outdoors, the tree can receive as much sun as you like, provided the pot is shaded and the soil is not allowed to become even slightly dry. In winter, it can be left outside in all weathers if sheltered from the wind and temperatures do not fall below -5°C (23°F). If colder, move to a frost-free shed or garage.

The strong yet graceful trunk of this Chinese hackberry provides a good base for the well-distributed branches and neat leaves.

Maintenance

Repotting Every year in spring for younger trees; every two years for older. Use Akadama or standard soil mix with a little extra coarse organic matter or calcined clay to increase water retention. (Provide extra shade and be extra-vigilant with watering if using Akadama.)

Pruning Branches can be pruned between leaf-fall and spring. Thin out congested areas and shorten overextended growth in mid-summer to induce rapid replacement growth, or in the dormant season for permanent removal.

Pinching Pinch out tips of new shoots when two true leaves have formed.

Watering Water copiously when in growth so never dry. In winter, maintain soil evenly moist.

Feeding Balanced feed in spring, followed by low-nitrogen for the rest of the growing season. Apply one nitrogen-free feed in autumn.

Beware! Although hackberry need permanently moist soil, they react badly to overwatering. Adding extra organic matter or water-retentive calcined clay to the soil will help.

Chaenomeles
Flowering Quince

Outdoor

This garden shrub has long been one of the most popular late winter/early spring-flowering plants in temperate regions the world over, with its apple-blossom-like flowers, ranging from pink to deep red with yellow centres.

Its natural multi-stemmed habit is caused by its tendency to produce suckers – adventitious shoots that grow from the spreading roots. This habit persists when quince is grown in a pot, which makes training it as a single-trunked tree very difficult, and the commercial examples are more trouble than they are worth.

Bonsai artists work with nature to produce a type of clump style unique to this species. After several years' growth in the ground, the plant is lifted and planted in a pot with the thick upper roots fully exposed. This also exposes the points of origin of the many suckers. Some are selected for training into trunks and the rest are pruned away. The trunks are trained by hard pruning to side growth every summer, which produces gnarled, angular trunks and short, stubby branches laden with flowering spurs.

Where to keep flowering quince

Quince thrive in full sun or in semi-shade, but they are not drought tolerant, so shade the pot on hot days. My quince spends the entire winter outdoors and has survived temperatures of -17°C (1.5°F) unscathed. Keep above -5°C (23°F) at night and give it plenty of sunshine during the day to encourage earlier flowering.

Maintenance

Repotting Every one to two years in spring for younger trees; every three to four years for older. Use standard soil mix with a little extra coarse organic matter and a deep pot.

ABOVE Regular hard pruning each year eventually produces gnarled, angular branches covered in masses of flower buds.

LEFT From Christmas through to late spring, the blossoms of flowering quince will reward you with a blaze of colour.

Pruning Prune for branch structure straight after flowering and allow all new shoots to grow unchecked until they stop extending – usually mid- to late summer. At this point, cut hard back, leaving only the first two or three leaves. It is the buds in the axils of these leaves that will develop into new flowering spurs.

Pinching Snip back late-season growth to one or two leaf nodes in autumn.

Watering Water copiously when in growth so never dry. In winter, maintain soil evenly moist.

Feeding Balanced feed in spring, followed by low-nitrogen for the rest of the growing season. Apply one nitrogen-free feed in autumn.

Beware! Chaenomeles bonsai are thirsty and wilt if the soil dries. This can cause the new shoots to wither and die. Aphids love quince.

Chamaecyparis obtusa
Hinoki Cypress

Outdoor

In nature, a hinoki cypress has a flame-shaped profile, but as the tree reaches maturity, it adopts a broad, almost domed appearance with clouds of foliage supported above branches that have become bare and exposed. This is the image that most hinoki bonsai try to evoke, although their slow-growing nature means that good examples are rare and expensive. More reasonably priced trees are still worth trying.

The scale-like leaves are edged with silvery-blue and the shoots curl inwards at the tips. The dense, compact shoots rapidly form clouds of foliage, which must be regularly pinched during the growing season. Periodically, all dead leaves and shoots should be cleaned away and the central spine of all clusters of shoots cut back to two healthy side shoots. Failure to do this will lead to long, meandering branches with tufts of green at the tips. Congested foliage is also perfect for red spider mites, which can devastate a tree in just a few weeks.

Where to keep hinoki cypress

Although tolerant of hot sun in the wild, in containers hinoki cypress are more happy in semi-shade during the hottest months. Hinoki can withstand frozen roots for considerable periods, provided the tree is not exposed to drying winds. The waxy coating provides some protection against wind, but not enough for containerized plants. It does, however, help the foliage to appear healthy long after the tree has died! Don't bring hinoki cypress into the house in winter – not even for an hour.

Most commercial chamaecyparis bonsai are created from dwarf varieties which readily produce sturdy trunks and masses of compact foliage.

Maintenance

Repotting Every two to three years in mid-spring; older specimens every five years. Use standard soil mix. Akadama can be used if you can guarantee never to let it dry out.

Pruning Prune branches and thin old twigs in summer, when wounds will heal easily and any knocked-off foliage will regrow quickly.

Pinching Pinch out the growing tips of all shoots as soon as they begin to overextend and spoil the tree outline. Repeat as necessary, spraying regularly for a week after each session.

Watering Hinoki cypress will not tolerate dry roots, and once they have been damaged by drought, they rarely recover. Water well all year, especially in summer, and avoid waterlogging.

Feeding Balanced feed from spring until late summer; nitrogen-free in early autumn. A dose of balanced, slow-release fertilizer in winter will prepare for spring. Apply all at half strength.

Beware! The fans of foliage on hinoki cypress are very easily dislodged when wiring or thinning out old twigs, so handle with care.

Cotoneaster horizontalis
Cotoneaster

Outdoor

Nearly everything the bonsai enthusiast wants is offered by this popular garden shrub. It has very small, glossy, dark green leaves that turn shades of orange or red in autumn. In spring, the tiny, spherical flowers cover the tree with a mass of pink and white. Later in the year, bright orange or red berries are borne prolifically, right through winter if the birds don't get them.

In spring, or after pruning, a new straight shoot will grow from every single leaf axil which, over the years, creates a uniform herringbone pattern of twigs. This enables even the beginner to predict exactly where each new shoot will grow from and its direction, making the development of good branch structures and neat, well-organized foliage clouds an almost boringly straightforward operation.

But there are two drawbacks. First, the growth of new shoots is so prolific that the regular trimming can become tedious. Second, the trunks and exposed roots are slow to thicken once the tree is growing in a container. If you are not satisfied with the thickness of the trunk, plant it in the ground for a couple of years.

A similar variety, *Cotoneaster microphyllus*, has evergreen leaves and white flowers that open completely like miniature apple blossom.

Where to keep cotoneaster

Full sun all year round suits cotoneasters perfectly. However, cotoneasters can be kept in semi-shade without any problems, but the fruit may not set quite so well. They can also be displayed indoors for a few days at a time at any time of year without coming to any harm. In winter, you can leave cotoneasters outside in most weathers, provided they are sheltered from persistent rain and winds. If the temperature dips below -7°C (19°F) for more than a day, take the tree into a shed or garage.

Maintenance

Repotting Mid-spring every one to two years; older, larger specimens every three years. Use standard soil mix with 20 per cent extra grit.

Pruning Prune branches, improve branch structure and thin overgrown spurs in spring, three weeks after repotting. Seal all wounds immediately to keep out fungal spores, particularly coral spot which can attack live tissue on this species. Prune away unwanted adventitious shoots as soon as they appear.

Pinching Pinching and trimming a large cotoneaster bonsai is almost a full-time occupation. Use sharp, pointed scissors to cut out all vigorous shoots completely. Other, less vigorous shoots should be cut back to two or three leaves, which will gradually build up a network of short spurs. It is tempting to just trim the foliage like a hedge, but this 'random pruning' does not allow you to control the growth pattern and structure of the branches.

Watering Cotoneasters are frequently used by gardeners to cover dry banks where little else will grow. In containers, they are rather less happy in dry soil, but will suffer root rot if the soil is wet. Water only when the soil is on the dry side in summer. Keep the soil barely moist in winter; shelter from persistent winter rain.

Feeding Balanced feed from spring until late summer, then nitrogen-free in early autumn.

Beware! Cotoneasters contain a toxin that is highly poisonous to some other plants. Clean tools after use with methylated spirits.

Cotoneaster is a perfect species for smaller bonsai. The minute leaves and colourful flowers and berries give year-round value.

Cryptomeria japonica
Japanese Cedar

Outdoor

Cryptomerias are tall, elegant trees with wide, shallow pads of foliage sitting on top of horizontal, fan-shaped branch structures. The needle-like leaves densely clothe the fleshy shoots, which curl downwards when young, unable to support the weight of foliage. As the shoots mature, they stiffen and are held erect.

As a response to pruning and regular pinching, abundant adventitious shoots emerge from twig and branch intersections. These are used to replace old and congested twigs that are periodically thinned out.

Like all conifers, cryptomeria branches are supple and bend easily, but if bent just a little too far they suddenly snap, so follow the guidelines given for *Carpinus* (see page 80). If a branch does snap during wiring, it won't break off entirely but will remain attached by a sliver of bark and wood. Cut off the wire, reassemble the branch and bind it tightly with raffia, sealing the whole area with cut paste. The branch should survive, but there will always be a weak point, so remember where the break was and avoid bending again at that point.

In winter, the foliage changes to a bronze or brown tint. This may look as if the tree is dying, but it is a perfectly normal reaction to the change in season. The foliage returns to its green colour as the weather improves in spring. This is the signal that it is time to repot.

Where to keep Japanese cedar

In their native Japan, cryptomerias inhabit the lower slopes of mountains where they are shrouded in mist in the morning and exposed to the sun for the rest of the day. Provided you can ensure that the pot will not dry out through evaporation and you can spray the foliage two or three times a day, your cryptomerias will do well in full sun. If you are not so confident, try semi-shade, but ensure that the tree has good overhead light. In winter, protect only from wind and prolonged periods of heavy frost.

Maintenance

Repotting Repot younger trees every two years in mid-spring; older and larger specimens every five years. Use the standard soil mix.

Pruning Prune branches and improve branch structure in late summer, while the tree still has time to begin healing before winter but it is too late for adventitious growth. Thin out congested areas in spring and pull out all unwanted adventitious growth as it appears.

Pinching Pinch out the tips of all new shoots while still soft and the needles are pale green. Do so every week in the growing season.

Watering Cryptomerias like cool, moist roots, so water well during the growing season, but not so often that the soil is permanently saturated. In winter, only water when the soil appears to be drying out.

Feeding Balanced feed from spring until late summer, followed by nitrogen-free in early autumn and a slow-release organic feed in mid-winter to nourish the spring growth.

Beware! The dense foliage provides a haven for red spider mites, which suck the sap from the fine shoots and the bases of leaves, causing large areas to turn brown and die back. Clean out all old foliage, and spray daily with cold water and monthly with insecticide as a preventative measure.

It takes many years for a young cryptomeria to reach this stage of development, with all the branches neatly organized and trimmed, but it's worth the wait.

Cycas
Cycad

Indoor & Outdoor

Cycads are among the most ancient species on earth, forming the link between ferns and trees in the evolutionary process. They are true tropicals that thrive on heat and humidity, and cannot cope with dry conditions. The first hint of dry roots will cause immediate loss of foliage and the plant is likely to deteriorate until it dies.

Although not strictly trees, cycads can be enjoyable to grow as bonsai since they evoke images of tropical islands. Try displaying the pot in a shallow tray filled with moist pebbles.

When buying, check that the growing tip in the centre of the fronds is green and healthy.

Where to keep cycad

The hotter and more humid, the better. Cycads will be happy in full sun outdoors in summer, provided they have been very gradually acclimatized, but changing their position is always risky. Indoors, the sun through glass is too intense, so provide light shade such as an open-weave net curtain. Some enthusiasts find that by placing their plants in a west-facing window the need for shade is eliminated.

Maintenance

Repotting Cycads are intolerant of excessive disturbance to the roots, which are thick and fleshy, and very easily damaged. Normal root pruning is out of the question. Fortunately, they are extremely slow growing, so only need repotting every five years at most. Increase the size of the pot at each repotting without disturbing the roots at all. Use a cactus compost.

Pruning Since there are no branches, conventional pruning does not apply. Dead fronds should be cut off – not pulled – close to the stem using a sharp knife. Angle the cut so that it slopes downwards away from the stem to produce the diamond-patterned texture familiar on the trunks of palm trees.

Pinching Don't pinch out the growing tip at any time. At best, this will distort the plant; at worst, it might kill it.

Watering In winter, the growth becomes slower, with the corresponding reduction in water uptake, so if the soil is already wet, there is no need to water. If the soil remains saturated for too long in winter, it may become stagnant.

Feeding Feed gently with balanced fertilizer all year round, reducing the strength in winter. Mild feeds such as fish emulsion can be used as directed; others should be used at half strength.

Beware! Cycads are very sensitive to changes in their local environment. After a sudden drop in local temperature, the fronds will turn yellow and fall. Draught, reduction in humidity and reduced light levels will have a similar effect. If this happens, move to a warm, bright location and keep the roots warm and slightly moist.

Cycads can bring an air of sun-drenched tropical islands into your home – especially welcome when the weather outside is cold and foggy.

Fagus crenata
Japanese Beech

Indoor & Outdoor

This is the only variety of beech used for commercial bonsai production. The smooth, pale grey bark persists throughout the tree's life, so the image of a mature tree can be established in a relatively young bonsai. When cleaned with an old toothbrush, the bark can appear almost white, which contrasts particularly well with the copper-coloured leaves in winter. The neat, slightly crinkly-edged, pointed leaves are borne on slender shoots.

In autumn, the leaves on a bonsai that has been shaded during high summer will turn yellow, then coppery brown. If exposed to too much sun, the leaves bypass the yellow phase.

If you want to remove the leaves, which often remain in winter, to wire train the branches, cut through the petioles rather than pulling away, to avoid damage to the delicate buds.

Where to keep Japanese beech

Beech can be kept in full sun for much of the time, but in high summer it may cause the leaves to become paler and adopt a leathery surface, which renders them less efficient at manufacturing essential sugars. Provide some shade during the hottest part of the year and return the tree to full sun as autumn approaches. Beech tolerate freezing well; only move to a shed or garage if temperatures remain below -7°C (19°F) for more than a week.

Maintenance

Repotting Every two to three years in spring. You can repot in autumn provided you can keep the tree more or less frost-free until spring – minimum -2°C (28°F). Use standard soil or Akadama. If using Akadama, be especially vigilant with watering during the first three months while new roots are being established.

Beech are sturdy trees with pale grey bark and copper-coloured autumn foliage, which remains on the tree until spring to protect the buds.

Pruning Prune the branches in late winter or early spring, three weeks before or after repotting. Pruning in mid-summer will aid vigorous regeneration from around the wound.

Pinching Pinch out the growing tips once two true leaves have begun to harden. Alternatively, to build up vigour in weak areas, allow the shoots to extend for six or seven leaves and then cut back to two.

Watering Water well during the growing season and keep moist in winter. In really hot weather, water twice a day as necessary.

Feeding Balanced feed during the growing season; nitrogen-free feed in late summer and autumn. Delay the first spring feed until three weeks after the buds have opened.

Beware! Beech leaves scorch easily when exposed to drying winds and can become pale and inefficient in strong sun. Although full-size trees can tolerate these conditions to a certain extent, trees in containers cannot, so protect from wind and sun at all times.

Ficus
Fig

Outdoor

Ficus retusa and *F. benjamina* are both native to Southeast Asia and are jungle plants. *F. microphylla* (small-leaved) comes from Australia and inhabits more exposed areas.

Figs all have in common a habit of producing aerial roots from branches and the upper trunk. In nature, the aerial roots growing from the branches eventually become strong enough to support the parent branch, structurally and nutritionally. Those emerging from the trunk tend to self-graft to the trunk as they grow downwards. This causes the trunk to thicken rapidly and adopt a deeply fluted appearance.

Large specimen bonsai figs use this natural process to good effect, but smaller ones are not vigorous enough for the self-grafting process to take place. If you want to develop your fig into a larger specimen, plant it in a bigger container and keep it in a warm, bright and humid place. Feed well and allow all shoots to grow to about ten leaves before hard pruning to leave just one or two leaves. After four or five years, it should be large enough for the aerial roots to self-graft when it is replanted into a larger bonsai pot.

Where to keep a fig

Although in nature many figs grow in full sun, most are ideally suited to life in the dappled shade of taller trees with sparse foliage, where their roots are in cooler, humus-rich soil and the surrounding air is humid. Keep your figs in good light but protected from direct sun, even if placed outdoors in summer.

Moving figs around or exposing them to draughts or dry air can cause the older leaves to turn yellow and fall. So once you have found a position that suits your bonsai, leave it there, turning it around once a week to ensure that it receives an even amount of light on all sides.

The roots of *Ficus* varieties are thick and fleshy, and quickly bond together when allowed to touch. This characteristic is often used to good effect, as with this interesting specimen.

Maintenance

Repotting Every two to three years in winter, or any other time with care. Keep the pot warm after root pruning to aid rapid regeneration of roots. Never water straight after repotting or all the leaves will drop. Use the standard soil mix.

Pruning Prune in winter when the sap flow is reduced. Figs 'bleed' a milky sap profusely from pruning wounds at all times of the year. The trees respond well to hard pruning.

Pinching Pinch out the growing tips once two true leaves have formed.

Watering Water well during the growing season and keep moist in winter. In really hot weather, water trees in very shallow containers twice a day as necessary.

Feeding Balanced feed during the growing season, reduced to half strength in winter.

Beware! The bark on most varieties swells rapidly when the plant is growing and is being well watered. This can cause wire to make scars within a few weeks. Check all wire regularly and remove it as soon as it appears too tight, reapplying afterwards if necessary.

Ginkgo biloba
Ginkgo

Outdoor

Ginkgos are the oldest of all trees alive today and are closely related to ferns. Once thought to be extinct, they were rediscovered in China in the 17th century.

The natural shape of ginkgos is tall and columnar. The trunks and branches become quite gnarled with age, but never develop a refined structure. They also resent pruning. Frequently pruned shoots will die back, sometimes right back to the parent branch. A branch with many pruned shoots may, in turn, die back to the trunk. In bonsai, the aim is to produce a characterful trunk onto which sufficient foliage-bearing shoots will grow each year to nourish the plant. To minimize die-back, leave a short stub and seal it immediately.

Ginkgos have a habit of growing vigorously one year and hardly at all the next. They also tend to abort some shoots in winter, which makes attempts at wire training futile. Ginkgos, therefore, are generally grown for their vivid yellow autumn colour, not their shape.

Where to keep ginkgo

Ginkgos are happy in full sun or partial shade. Sun will improve autumn colour, but if the soil is allowed to dry out through evaporation the tree will respond by aborting shoots and branches. Shade prevents this but encourages leggy growth and large leaves. Finding the right location is a case of trial and error. Protection from all but light frost is mandatory. Never bring a ginkgo into the house in winter.

Ginkgos naturally form tall, conical trees that become gnarled and twisted with age. This bonsai specimen is already beginning to display the same character.

Maintenance

Repotting Every year in late winter or early spring. Use very sharp tools to avoid crushing the fleshy roots. Use standard soil mix with a little extra moisture-retentive organic matter.

Pruning Prune branches and old shoots in late spring, three or more weeks after repotting, when the swelling buds will indicate which shoots have survived the winter.

Pinching Pinch out the growing tips once two true leaves have formed.

Watering Water well during the growing season and keep just moist in winter. Spray foliage regularly.

Feeding Balanced feed during the growing season; nitrogen-free in autumn.

Beware! The thick fleshy roots contain a large quantity of water that expands on freezing and can burst the roots – especially dangerous when there is an imbalance of moisture between the roots and surrounding soil. So protect from prolonged or severe freezing.

Ilex crenata
Japanese Holly

Indoor & Outdoor

This deciduous tree has tiny oval leaves that turn anything from yellow, through orange to red in autumn. If fertilized by a nearby male tree, it will produce masses of small red berries, which can remain until the following spring.

The bark is quite thick and fleshy, so wiring must be done with great care. Wire when the soil is on the dry side so that the branches will bend a little more easily and the bark is less likely to be damaged. It may take a year or two for the branches to set in position. Check regularly that the wire is not scarring the bark as it swells, especially at the top of the tree. As soon as the wire appears too tight, remove it and reapply, coiling in the opposite direction.

Where to keep Japanese holly

Japanese holly is one of the very few species that can be kept indoors or outdoors, in sun or shade. It requires a dormant period in winter – moving it into an unheated room will suffice. In summer, it will appreciate fresh air through an open window and a misting with cool water two or three times a day. Outdoors, if kept in sun, don't allow the roots to dry out. The growth will be slower and the leaves smaller on trees exposed to the sun. Autumn colour is improved by placing in shade during summer and acclimatizing it to the sun in early autumn.

Maintenance

Repotting Every two to three years in late winter or early spring. Use the standard soil mix or Akadama.

Pruning Prune branches and old shoots in late spring, before the buds have opened. Alternatively, prune in autumn and keep the tree frost-free all winter. Hollow wounds to prevent the healing tissues forming unsightly swellings. Hard prune in summer to regenerate vigorous growth on weak branches.

Pinching Pinch out the growing tips once flowering is over. Trim lightly to shape as necessary during the rest of the growing season.

Watering Water well during the growing season and keep just moist in winter. Spray foliage regularly in warm weather.

Feeding Balanced feed during the growing season; nitrogen-free in autumn.

Beware! When you see a Japanese holly covered with berries in the nursery, it is a female tree. Don't be misled into thinking that it will be covered in fruit again next year – it won't unless you buy a male tree to fertilize it.

The colourful berries of Japanese holly delight the birds as well as the eye! If you want to enjoy your bonsai in fruit, keep it under bird netting from late summer onwards.

Juniperus chinensis
Chinese Juniper

Outdoor

Chinese junipers can be shaped to almost any style. This superb cascade style depicts a tree clinging to life on a mountain ledge.

In the mountains of Japan, these tough trees adopt gnarled and twisted trunks and branches with large areas of exposed 'driftwood'; this habit is generally echoed in bonsai. Provided you leave sufficient foliage to sustain the plant, you have total creative freedom in making your own jins and sharis to improve or even entirely redesign your bonsai.

With regular pinching, the densely borne shoots rapidly form a neat, clearly defined silhouette. Periodically, the foliage should be thinned out and the silhouette rebuilt with younger shoots that constantly emerge from branch intersections in healthy plants. The outer bark, which is grey-brown and flaky, can be carefully peeled off to reveal the smooth orange-red under-bark, which contrasts beautifully with the rich green foliage and the silvery-white jins and sharis.

Juniper branches are notoriously slow to set after wiring. The springy, resinous nature of the heartwood, the relatively thin layers of xylem deposited each year and their unusual longevity combine to make juniper bonsai the most time-consuming of all. Young branches up to 5 mm (¼ in) thick on young trees may set in a year or two, but older branches, especially on older trees, may never set. It is common to see masterpiece juniper bonsai exhibited in Japan with every branch wired.

Where to keep Chinese juniper

Junipers do well in full sun, producing neat, compact foliage. If placed in semi-shade, the growth will be slower to start in spring but the colour will be somewhat richer.

There is no need to protect your juniper from frost. Cold wind may cause the foliage to turn bronze, but it will turn green again in spring.

Maintenance

Repotting Every two to five years in mid-spring. Use the standard soil mix with an extra 20 per cent finely chopped fresh sphagnum moss (the sort used to line hanging baskets).

Pruning Prune branches and old shoots in late summer when the sap is not rising too fast and 'bleeding' is less of a problem.

Pinching Pinch out all the growing tips with the fingers to keep a neat silhouette. Vigorous extension shoots should be cut back as far as possible to a healthy side shoot or removed. Clean foliage from the undersides of branches.

Watering Water well during the growing season; keep just moist in winter. Although drought tolerant, junipers can consume a large amount of water, especially during winter.

Feeding Balanced feed during the growing season; nitrogen-free in autumn. An additional dose of slow-release balanced feed in mid-winter will strengthen spring growth.

Beware! In the wild, junipers naturally shed branches from time to time in order to maintain a balance between the efficiency of the roots and the demands of the foliage. This also happens with container-grown plants.

Juniperus rigida
Needle Juniper

Outdoor

Needle junipers are aptly named. The first thing you learn about them is that the needle-like leaves, borne in groups of three, are very sharp and take some getting used to! They can also be temperamental – losing shoots or branches, refusing to grow where you expect them to and so on. However, once established and growing well, needle junipers are one of the finest species for bonsai and good examples are much sought after by the connoisseur.

The young shoots are flaccid and droop downwards, temporarily giving the tree an untidy appearance. As they mature, they strengthen and hold themselves more upright, but they should be pinched back before they reach that stage. At the base of each needle is a tiny embryonic bud, which has the potential to grow into a new shoot. Light pinching will induce the two or three buds nearest to the tip to extend; harder pinching will induce a greater number of buds to extend and more adventitious shoots to emerge from two- or three-year-old wood.

It is essential to thin out congested areas of foliage every few years to allow light and air into the centre of the tree. Cut out old, woody spurs, leaving intact the fresh new growth from further down the branch. This will then be used to rebuild the foliage clouds.

Where to keep needle juniper

Needle junipers thrive in full sun. If they are grown in shade, the shoots become leggy, unable to support their own weight and prone to die-back. Place another bonsai or some other object close to the pot to shade the roots from the hot sun during mid-summer.

In winter, protect from prolonged or severe freezing to stop the foliage turning brown and

to ensure that the roots do not suffer. By the time you are aware of a problem with the roots, it may be too late to remedy it.

Maintenance

Repotting Every two to five years in mid-spring. Use standard soil with an additional 20 per cent grit, or Akadama.

Pruning Prune branches in late spring, but not in the same year as repotting. Use the stubs of pruned branches to shape into jins, or consider linking two jins with a shari (see pages 68–9). Thin out congested areas in summer.

Pinching Pinch out all the growing tips with the fingers to keep a neat silhouette. Vigorous extension shoots should be cut back to three or four needles. Clean all foliage from the undersides of branches.

Watering Water well during the growing season and keep just moist in winter. Avoid waterlogged soil at all costs.

Feeding Half-strength balanced feed during the growing season; nitrogen-free in autumn. An additional dose of slow-release balanced feed at half strength in mid-winter will strengthen spring growth.

Beware! Needle junipers have a reputation for dying without any apparent cause. The truth is that there is always a cause, but the metabolism of this species is so slow that a plant can be dead for a year or more before the foliage starts to dry off and the shoots stop extending.

The deadwood on this needle juniper already existed when it was gathered from the wild. The final image is that of a much taller conifer standing alone on a remote mountainside.

Lagerstroemia
Crape Myrtle

Indoor & Outdoor

The smooth bark of this crape myrtle will soon begin to flake away, revealing an ever-changing pattern of pinks and browns. With luck, it will also provide its owner with a flush of vivid flowers in late summer.

Originally from China and Korea, crape myrtles have become popular garden and hedging plants in Mediterranean and sub-tropical regions. They are grown mainly for their short-lived but flamboyant late-summer or early-autumn flowers, varying from lilac, through pinks to almost white. In bonsai culture, however, the plant can be reluctant to flower, but the bark is sufficiently striking to make it a worthwhile species for bonsai even without the flowers. As the bark ages, it peels away in irregular flakes revealing a different-coloured under-bark. This can vary from pale grey, through shades of rust and brown to almost pink, depending on the time of year. Spraying regularly with fresh water and exposure to the sun will encourage the bark to flake.

Where to keep crape myrtle

Full sun in summer, either close to an open window or outside on a balcony or windowsill. It will tolerate sun through glass. If leaving outside at night, acclimatize by gradually increasing the length of time spent outside each day. Choose a mild night for the first night out. In winter, reduce light levels and temperature to induce dormancy. Insufficient dormancy will induce premature spring growth and weaken the tree, as well as shorten the flowering period.

Maintenance

Repotting Every one to three years in mid-spring. Use standard bonsai soil.

Pruning Prune branches in autumn, hollowing out the wound to prevent swelling as it heals. Allow spring growth to extend until the leaves begin to harden and cut all shoots back to two or three leaves. The next crop of shoots will bear the flowers in late summer/autumn, and should not be trimmed until you are sure where the flower buds have formed.

Pinching If you want flowers, don't pinch out any growth until late summer when the flower buds will be visible and can be left. Pinch overextended shoots only to keep the tree neat.

Watering Water well during the growing season and sparingly when the tree is dormant. The swelling of the buds in spring will tell you that it is time to increase the water gradually.

Feeding To maximize flowering and to keep vigour under control, give regular low-nitrogen feeds throughout the growing period and one or two doses of nitrogen-free feed in autumn.

Beware! Crape myrtles must have a dormant period each winter to thrive. During this time, temperatures must be 7–10°C (45–50°F), and light and water kept to the bare minimum.

Ligustrum sinense
Chinese Privet

Indoor & Outdoor

All privets make excellent bonsai. Their glossy oval leaves are borne in pairs on straight shoots that emerge prolifically from young and old wood alike in response to pruning and pinching. They are strong growers and thrive in poor soils, requiring few nutrients. Although classed as evergreens, in temperate climates they become semi-evergreen. In very cold winters the foliage turns purple and some or all of the leaves may be shed, but when spring arrives the plant always bounces back with a new crop of vigorous shoots.

Where to keep Chinese privet

Chinese privet is extremely tough and versatile, and is one of the few species equally at home in a centrally heated house or out in the garden. If grown indoors, it will need as much light as possible all year round, but outside, privet will grow happily in sun or shade. However, when grown in shade, the leaves will be larger and more lush in colour and texture, but are more likely to fall in winter.

Maintenance

Repotting Every two to four years in mid-spring. It can be repotted as late as mid-summer if root disturbance is kept to a minimum. Use the standard soil mix or Akadama.

Pruning Prune branches in late spring or early summer. Thin out congested spurs in mid-summer and wire train all new shoots while they are still green.

Ever seen a privet like this? The dramatically raised roots give the impression of a tree growing at the edge of a raging river, where seasonal floods have eroded the topsoil.

Pinching Large bonsai can be allowed to grow unpinched from early summer to maximize flowering. With smaller bonsai, it is best to sacrifice the flowers and pinch back all new growth, as necessary, to keep the tree neat.

Watering Maintain even moisture in the soil throughout the year and never overwater. Dry soil can become difficult to re-wet, particularly if the organic matter used is peat based. Dry roots will cause lower branches to die back. Every two or three weeks, immerse the pot in a bowl of water so that the water is at the same level as the soil surface. When the surface looks wet, remove the pot and drain it thoroughly.

Feeding To keep vigour under control and to induce flowering, feed with low-nitrogen fertilizer throughout the growing season. A single dose of nitrogen-free feed in autumn will toughen plants kept outside.

Beware! Chinese privet cannot tolerate having dry roots for several days, but the roots will soon start to decay if conditions are too wet. The pot also rapidly fills with dense, fibrous roots, which can make water penetration slow.

Malus spp.
Crab Apple

Outdoor

There are countless varieties of crab apple used for bonsai, with blooms ranging from deep cerise, through shades of pink to almost pure white. On some, the flowers are followed by fruit, but it is good practice to remove these to divert more energy into producing flower buds.

Varieties of malus are grafted onto dwarfing root stocks because they are inefficient when growing on their own roots. Sometimes the graft union swells or leaves an obvious scar that gets worse as the tree ages, so take extra care when buying crab apple bonsai.

Where to keep crab apple

Crab apples adore sunshine, but perform less well when grown in shade. They can tolerate heavy freezing for long periods, although small bonsai in small containers may be more at risk. Bring indoors in spring for a day or so to admire the flowers, but return outside at night.

Maintenance

Repotting Every one to two years in autumn. Use a deeper than normal pot. Use standard soil mix with an extra 20 per cent organic matter or some granular clay-based soil.

Pruning Prune branches and all non-flowering last year's shoots back to a short stub, in late spring after flowering. Once the shape is established, maximize flowering by allowing all new growth to extend until mid- to late summer, then cut back all shoots to leave two to four flower buds at the base of the shoots.

Pinching Avoid pinching during early summer. Pinching will encourage vegetative growth at the expense of flowers. Only pinch out the tips of any overextending shoots produced in response to late-summer pruning.

Watering Water well in the growing season, particularly while the fruit is being formed. Keep moist but not wet in winter. Spray foliage and flowers regularly with fresh water.

Feeding Balanced feed in spring after flowering, then low-nitrogen in summer and nitrogen-free in autumn. Feed half strength administered twice as often.

Beware! Crab apples prefer a deeper pot than most species to ensure there is always an adequate supply of moisture and nutrients.

FAR LEFT Crab apple bonsai are pruned in late summer to induce prolific flowering the following spring.

LEFT Delicate crab apple blossom can vary from almost pure white through to deep pink.

Murraya paniculata
Jasmine Orange

Indoor

The fragrant white flowers and small orange fruit earned this native of India its common name, although it is not related to either jasmine or the citrus family. It has small, compound leaves that are held on stiff stems and produces new shoots from old wood after pruning. The bark is smooth and pale grey-brown when young, displaying more grey and breaking into fine vertical ridges as it ages.

To increase local humidity, spray jasmine orange regularly with fresh water and stand the pot in a tray of water, supported on stones to keep the drainage holes clear of the surface.

Although *Murraya* are not the easiest of species to keep indoors, the interesting bark textures and vigorous growth make the extra effort worthwhile.

Where to keep jasmine orange

Jasmine oranges are true tropicals that thrive in hot, steamy forests where there is ample rainfall and the temperature rarely falls below 17°C (63°F). Most homes have a room that can provide these conditions for most of the time, but it is not quite so easy to maintain jungle-like conditions all year round. If the tree's local environment is allowed to vary too often, its health will deteriorate.

A sunny windowsill in a kitchen or heated bathroom is perfect provided the window is not opened during the colder months.

Maintenance

Repotting Every two to four years in spring. Keep the pot warm after repotting to aid regeneration of the roots. Use the standard soil mix with an additional 30 per cent organic matter or granular clay-based soil.

Pruning Prune branches hard in early winter and seal wounds immediately to prevent further die-back. If die-back occurs, incorporate it into the design of the bonsai by creating

interesting hollows. Treat the exposed wood with lime-sulphur solution that has a little Indian ink added to tone down the colour.

Pinching Once the silhouette of the foliage clouds has been established, pinch out the growing tips of all extending shoots, leaving two or three leaves intact. Clean out dead twigs.

Watering Water well while in active growth and reduce water slightly when growth slows in winter. Never let the soil become dry. Immerse the pot in a bowl of water once a week. Spraying may cause the bark to swell and fall away.

Feeding Half-strength balanced feed through the year, provided the tree is in active growth. Withhold feed if growth ceases during winter.

Beware! The bark is quite thick and separates easily from the heartwood if handled carelessly. Too much pressure when wiring or the use of blunt tools when pruning will result in disaster. Watch out for mildew on plants subjected to poor air circulation, and aphids on all plants.

Myrtus apiculata
Myrtle

Indoor & Outdoor

Myrtle offers the bonsai enthusiast an opportunity to create a fine specimen in a relatively short time, with its vigorous growth, small shiny leaves and beautiful, tiny white flowers with golden centres. Most commercial myrtle bonsai tend to be modest in size and quality, but they do constitute excellent material to develop further. Occasionally, larger, more refined specimens appear in nurseries and are well worth the additional expense.

When buying, check that the roots have not deteriorated due to overwatering. Gently rock the tree in its pot – if unstable, don't buy it.

Where to keep myrtle

Myrtles are sub-tropicals, so they require warmth throughout the year but with slightly reduced temperatures in winter so that the tree can enter its rest period. In fact, in summer it cannot be too hot for myrtles. They adore heat and relatively high humidity, but are not so happy if exposed to direct sun through glass.

If kept indoors all year round, place near a sunny window where it will be shaded from afternoon sun. Outdoors in summer it can be exposed to full sun, but the pot should be shaded to prevent the roots from overheating. Maintain winter temperatures at about 5–7°C (41–45°F) and keep away from cold draughts.

Maintenance

Repotting Every two to three years in spring. Take care not to cut too far into the old roots. If you want to reduce the heavier roots, do so over a number of years. Use the standard soil mix, with ericaceous (lime-free) compost for the organic content. Myrtles sometimes lose their leaves after root pruning, and they can take a long time to regrow, so be patient.

Myrtles produce an abundance of shoots and flowers, making them ideal subjects for bonsai specimens and as popular in the West as they are in their native China.

Pruning You can prune your myrtle at any time of year but it is best done while resting.

Pinching Use sharp nail scissors to trim the foliage clouds to shape whenever the tree looks untidy. The hundreds of adventitious shoots produced from all parts of the branches and trunk must be painstakingly removed by pulling them away cleanly. If you try to cut these off, you will leave a short stub from which many more shoots will rapidly appear.

Watering Water carefully in the growing period, keeping the soil moist but not saturated. In winter, keep the watering to a minimum – just enough to prevent the soil from becoming completely dry. Spray with fresh water daily.

Feeding Half-strength balanced feed only while the tree is in active growth.

Beware! Myrtles are calcifuges – lime-haters – and will slowly deteriorate if supplied with hard tap water. Use collected rainwater whenever possible and treat with a proprietary soil acidifier three or four times a year.

Nandina domestica
Nandina/Heavenly Bamboo

Indoor & Outdoor

Nandina is an attractive subject for cultivation in shallow containers. It has bamboo-like leaves that emerge deep red and often remain that colour for several months, particularly in good light. The small, whitish flowers are borne in loose spikes and are followed by bright red berries. Its habit of producing a multitude of new shoots from ground level means that it is particularly difficult to create a trunk of any worth, so the ideal style for this species is a clump or grove. After a number of years, the base may become woody, and it can then be exposed by raising the plant in its pot. Constant hard pruning of old stems will eventually add much character, or you can encourage the clump to spread sideways by selective pruning and division.

Where to keep heavenly bamboo

Nandinas are happy to spend all year in most normal domestic environments provided air circulation is good and there is sufficient light, but not in direct sunlight. However, they will benefit from spending the warmer months outside in semi-shade. If kept indoors in summer, place near an open window to ensure good air circulation and spray twice a day with fresh water. Nandinas must not experience temperatures below 7°C (45°F).

Maintenance

Repotting Every three to four years in spring. Clumps can be divided at repotting time, to create additional plantings or to increase the size of the existing one by spreading it out in a larger container. Use the standard soil mix with an additional 30 per cent organic matter.

Pruning Prune old stems right back to ground level or to the old, woody stump-like base. Thin the many new shoots to prevent overcrowding.

Pinching Snip off the tips of side shoots to maintain an overall neat appearance. Take care not to trim off the flowering shoots, which usually emerge in early summer from a near-apical bud on last year's growth.

Watering Keep the soil moist at all times, but avoid waterlogging.

Feeding Low-nitrogen fertilizer throughout the growing period.

Beware! Young nandinas are not strong and are less resilient than older examples. The shock of transportation from the Far East and the consequent change of growing conditions can seriously damage a young plant. Avoid small nandinas that display any sign of weakness.

Nandinas are similar to bamboo although they are not related in any way. The leaves adopt a beautiful rich red colour when kept in good light.

Olea europaea
Olive

Indoor

Olives can be easily transplanted, even when very old. This enables commercial bonsai producers to collect wild material of significant size and age, and some very fine specimen bonsai are now available at reasonable cost. Although olives are slow-growing, the shoots can extend rapidly in spring and early autumn. Their natural habit is to shut down during high summer when, in the wild, it is too hot and dry for growth to take place. The white shoots are very rigid and grow in all directions. If you want to wire them, do so while they are still growing and not yet too brittle.

Where to keep olive

Olives prefer full sun all day, every day. They are extremely drought tolerant, so you don't need to worry too much if the heat of the sun completely dries out the soil from time to time. When watered after drought, olives consume vast amounts of water to be stored in the fleshy leaves and bark. They should be considered as tender when grown in containers. Protect from temperatures below 5°C (41°F).

Maintenance

Repotting Every three years or so – olives can live happily without repotting for up to a decade, but it is good practice to repot fairly regularly so that you can inspect the general health of the plant. Use a mix of 30 per cent organic matter to 70 per cent grit.

Pruning Prune in early autumn or early spring using a fine-toothed saw to cope with the extremely hard wood. Olives do not regenerate new growth from immediately behind the wound on shortened branches. The stubs invariably die right back to their point of origin and any new growth stimulated by the pruning will emerge from the trunk or the parent branch. Shorten branches in stages, saving the final cut until there are conveniently placed side shoots to prune back to.

Pinching The shoots are too tough for finger pinching, so use sharp nail scissors to trim wayward shoots back to two or three leaves.

Watering Keep the soil just moist enough to sustain the plant by watering heavily but infrequently; more infrequently in winter. Spray with fresh water in very hot weather.

Feeding Half-strength solution of balanced feed throughout summer and one nitrogen-free feed in autumn. Do not feed in winter.

Beware! Olive branches have little tolerance of bending and snap at the base very easily, or they often die back after wiring. But new shoots grow in all directions and it is usually possible to shape a branch by selective pruning alone.

Olives have only recently been developed as subjects for commercial bonsai production, so mature specimens are very rare. However, charming young bonsai like this are rapidly becoming popular.

Pinus parviflora (P. pentaphylla)
Japanese White Pine

Outdoor

Japanese white pines are the most dainty and elegant of all pines. Their small needles, borne in groups of five, are green on the underside and have silvery-white lines along the centres of the other two sides, which gives the impression of the tree being bathed in a pale blue haze. The bark remains smooth until the tree is very old, so commercial bonsai are invariably grafted onto black pine trunks, which develop deep fissures much sooner. The graft is made just below the lowest branch, so the foliage covers the obvious change in bark texture. If you should spot an ungrafted white pine with flaky bark right to the apex, snap it up.

On established bonsai, the old needles should be pulled out in late summer, to allow light and air into the branches to strengthen inner growth, and to control the distribution of energy to different parts of the tree. Pull out more needles on the upper shoots, leaving four or five clusters intact. Increase the number of needles remaining to seven or eight clusters in the centre of the tree, and ten or so on the lower branches. On the weakest branches, clean out dead or dying needles. This ensures that the tree's energy is not concentrated in the apex.

Where to keep white pine

White pines are designed to spend their summers in full sun and fresh air, so they only tolerate being indoors for a day or so. In semi-shade, the foliage loses its silvery sheen. In winter, protect from persistent temperatures below -5°C (23°F) and cold winds.

Maintenance

Repotting Every two to five years in late spring. Be careful not to tear at the roots when you untangle them. A white fluffy substance around

The blue-green needles of white pine are borne in closely set groups of five, giving even a young plant a dense canopy. This older specimen boasts a long, sweeping lower branch, typical of trees growing on lower mountain slopes.

the roots is a beneficial mycorrhizal fungus that helps the tree digest nutrients. Use a mix of 30 per cent organic matter to 70 per cent grit, or Akadama with 20 per cent grit added.

Pruning Prune in late summer to early autumn when the wounds are less likely to bleed resin, which stains the bark an undesirable white. Seal wounds immediately.

Pinching Break off the tips of the new shoots as they extend.

Watering Keep the soil moist but try never to saturate it. Pines prefer very free-draining soil, so, to be safe, shelter from prolonged rainfall.

Feeding Half-strength solution of balanced feed throughout summer and one nitrogen-free feed in autumn, plus a single application of slow-release organic fertilizer in mid-winter.

Beware! White pines are reluctant to produce adventitious buds on older wood, without which the branches cannot be restructured. Regular feeding, needle pulling and shoot pinching is essential. When you do spot an adventitious bud, treasure it and wait a year or so before asking it to replace an older part of the branch that you want to prune away.

Pinus thunbergii
Japanese Black Pine

Outdoor

Black pines are common parkland trees in their native Japan. Their tolerance of poor, dry soils and harsh pruning make them suitable even for planting in the centres of motorway intersections and in busy city streets. They are even seen growing in the crevices between the walls of adjacent houses. The needles are a shiny, rich green and stand erect in pairs from the stout shoots. The charcoal-grey bark develops deep fissures in quite young trees and the branches thicken and mature in a relatively short time. Together, these produce a strong, masculine tree, full of rugged character.

The needles are, if anything, a little longer than would be ideal. With strong, healthy trees, the water can be reduced to absolute minimum at the point in late spring when the needles are about half size and beginning to stand away from the elongating 'candle'. This will arrest the development of the needles. Once the needles have hardened and are standing erect from the shoot, normal watering can be resumed and the needles will not extend. This routine can be repeated in alternate years.

Where to keep black pine

Black pines are designed to spend their summers in full sun and fresh air, so they only tolerate being indoors for a day or so, and never in winter. In semi-shade, the growth is weak and budding is poor. In winter, protect only from persistent temperatures below -5°C (23°F), excessive rain and cold winds.

Japanese black pines are strong trees with dark, craggy bark and bright green needles. This ancient specimen has a superbly shaped trunk and excellent branch structure.

Maintenance

Repotting Every two to five years in late spring. Be careful not to tear at the roots when you untangle them. If you see a white fluffy substance around the roots, you're in luck. This is a beneficial mycorrhizal fungus that helps the tree digest nutrients. Root aphids also appear white and fluffy, but they move! Use a mix of 20 per cent organic matter to 80 per cent grit, or Akadama with 30 per cent grit added.

Pruning Prune in late summer to early autumn when the wounds are less likely to bleed resin, which stains the bark white. Seal wounds immediately. When removing branches, consider leaving a stub and shaping it into a jin. Keep the branches in proportion by pruning back the outer twigs to healthy adventitious shoots, which appear on older wood. These can then be wire trained and grown on to replace the outer twigs until they too will eventually be pruned back and the process is repeated.

Pinching Break off the tips of the new shoots as they extend and pull out all old needles in late summer (see pages 63–4 for detailed information on pinching and needle pulling for pines).

Watering Keep the soil moist, but don't saturate it. Pines prefer very free-draining soil, so, to be safe, it is best to shelter them from prolonged rainfall.

Feeding Half-strength solution of balanced feed throughout summer and one nitrogen-free feed in autumn, plus a single application of slow-release organic fertilizer in mid-winter.

Beware! Black pines are prone to root rot if the soil remains wet for too long. To avoid this problem, ensure that the soil is very free-draining and shelter the tree from prolonged rainfall, especially in winter.

Pistacia terebinthus
Pistachio

Indoor

Pistachios are found in the Mediterranean region, and the Far East where commercial bonsai are produced. They are sub-tropical plants, never growing bigger than a large shrub.

The thick, glossy green, compound leaves are borne on stiff shoots and appear to grow in all directions, which makes it difficult to keep a small bonsai neat, so opt for a medium to large bonsai. In spring, when growth is most rapid, the bark thickens dramatically and the branches become brittle as they are pumped full of water. Wiring at this time is risky – the branches snap easily and the bark will separate from the heartwood with the slightest pressure, resulting in the death of the rest of the branch. It is better to shape branches by selective pruning, cutting back to a bud that faces in the direction you want the new shoot to grow.

Where to keep pistachio
Pistachios enjoy full sun when growing in open ground but are less tolerant of it when grown in pots, especially if the sun is intensified through window glass. If your pistachio lives indoors all summer, give it the maximum possible light without exposing it to hot afternoon sun. If it lives outdoors in summer, position where the pot is shaded from the afternoon sun.

Maintenance
Repotting Every three years or so – more often if the tree appears to be root-bound. The roots are easily crushed, so always use very sharp tools and avoid tearing at the roots when untangling them. Use the standard soil mix with some additional organic matter.

Pruning Pistachios can be pruned at any time of year. The fleshy bark separates easily from

Pistachios are fascinating little trees, with rigid shoots growing in all directions. Once tamed, they make dramatic bonsai and are a good species to experiment on.

the heartwood under pressure, so always use very sharp tools. Wounds heal quite quickly but occasionally die back, especially if the soil is a little on the dry side. Seal wounds immediately.

Pinching The shoots are too tough to pinch with the fingers, so use sharp nail scissors to snip them back to one or two leaves. The compound leaves can appear a little unkempt, so try cutting through the central stem of each leaf to leave just two of the leaflets. This will also help to promote back-budding.

Watering Keep the soil moist at all times, but don't allow it to remain saturated for long periods. Once a week, immerse the pot in a bowl of water for 20 minutes.

Feeding Balanced feed throughout summer and autumn. If temperatures are kept above 20°C (68°F) in winter, the tree might continue growing. If growth does continue, half-strength balanced fertilizer should be applied, but stop feeding as soon as growth ceases.

Beware! Pistachios will not tolerate dry roots, so cover the soil surface with moss or gravel to reduce evaporation. Stand the pot above a tray of water to increase local humidity and help reduce further moisture loss from the leaves.

Podocarpus macrophyllus
Chinese Yew

Indoor & Outdoor

This evergreen conifer is one of the most popular trees in ornamental gardens throughout the Far East. Its popularity is due to the rich, glossy foliage which persists for several years and becomes very dense.

In nature, the trunks of podocarpus tend to divide into several vertical branches at 1 m (3 ft) above the ground, each branch supporting several horizontal secondary branches bearing flat pads of dense foliage. This habit, if copied, can produce an extremely interesting bonsai.

Where to keep Chinese yew

Chinese yews enjoy sunshine, so keep your tree outdoors in summer where it will receive full sun all day long, provided you can shade the pot or cover the soil with moss to reduce moisture loss through evaporation. Indoors, the tree should be shaded from hot sun through glass during the hottest part of the day. Create a humid atmosphere by regular spraying and by standing the pot over a tray of water. To be safe, keep above 5°C (41°F) during winter.

Maintenance

Repotting Every three years or longer, in late spring. The roots are very sensitive to pruning, so only remove one-eighth of the root mass at any one time. Be very gentle when untangling the roots – the slightest damage will cause the tree to react badly and may result in loss of some shoots and branches. Water sparingly for the first few weeks after repotting to encourage

the new roots to extend rapidly in search of water. Use the standard soil mix or Akadama.

Pruning Branches can be pruned at any time during the growing period. Use very sharp tools at all times and be careful not to crush the bark as you cut. Chinese yews are slow to regenerate new growth from old wood, preferring to throw out new shoots from parts of the branches that still bear old foliage.

Pinching The shoots are too tough and fibrous and the foliage too dense for finger pinching. Use very sharp nail scissors to cut through the new shoots, leaving five or six new leaves.

Watering Water regularly in the growing period, reducing slightly in winter and after repotting. Spray foliage regularly with water.

Feeding Half-strength balanced feed in summer. If the tree is kept warm in winter, it will continue growing and feeding should continue, but stop feeding if growing ceases.

Beware! Chinese yews have extremely sensitive roots and react badly to root pruning. Overwatering turns leaves grey.

The foliage of this attractive little tree has an unmistakable Oriental appearance. Guy wires have been used to hold some stubborn branches in place until they set.

Punica granatum
Pomegranate

Indoor

The Romans were responsible for spreading this attractive small Mediterranean tree throughout the region because of its beautiful bell-shaped red or pink flowers and succulent fruit. Pomegranates are also native to China.

Pomegranates will lose some of or all their leaves in winter if temperatures fall below a certain point or if water is scarce. This is not a problem because the three most endearing features of this species are its flowers, fruit and bark. The bark is smooth buff to brown on young plants and buds soon develop a stringy texture as the tree matures. The main 'veins' linking the roots and branches swell at a greater rate than the rest of the bark and, eventually, the bark in the spaces between the veins dies. This creates a gnarled, ancient look to the tree.

Where to keep pomegranates
Pomegranates can be exposed to full sun all day long, indoors or out. During the hottest months of the year, it is advisable to shade the pots from sun through glass to prevent the roots from 'cooking'. If you want your pomegranate to remain evergreen, maintain winter temperatures above 17°C (63°F). Never allow the temperature to fall below 5°C (41°F)

LEFT The bright vermilion, trumpet-shaped flowers are borne in early summer.

FAR RIGHT Pomegranates have gnarled bark, twisted trunks, gorgeous flowers and fruit, and yellow autumn leaves. Who could ask for more from a bonsai?

and protect from cold draughts at all times. Give as much light as possible in winter.

Maintenance
Repotting Every two or three years in early spring, before growth starts; old plants up to five years. Use the standard soil mix or Akadama mixed with 30 per cent grit to ensure good drainage. Use a fairly deep pot.

Pruning Prune unwanted branches in spring. Hard prune all branches for structure straight after flowering, then allow all new shoots to grow unchecked until flower buds can be seen on the shorter, non-extending shoots. At this point, you can safely prune back the longer shoots to two or three leaves. These stubs will form the base for next year's flowering shoots.

Pinching The flowers are borne on short shoots emerging from last year's growth. Restrict pinching to shoots that are overextending during flowering. Pinching at any other time may restrict flowering.

Watering Water well at all times. Water consumption increases while fruit are swelling. In winter, reduce watering if the leaves fall.

Feeding Balanced feed until flowering commences, then cease feeding. Resume when flowering has finished with low-nitrogen fertilizer. If the tree remains in leaf during winter, give a weak dose of slow-release organic balanced feed. If your pomegranate is reluctant to flower, apply low-nitrogen fertilizer all summer and for as long into the autumn/winter as the tree remains in leaf.

Beware! The branches of pomegranates are very brittle, even when quite young. Wire train new shoots while they are still green and pliable, taking care not to create over-sharp angles, which will crush the inner tissue and cause the shoot to die.

Pyracantha
Firethorn

Outdoor

In late spring, firethorn explodes in a profusion of creamy-white flowers borne in flat panicles, standing above the branches. In late summer and autumn, the weight of the masses of orange or red berries causes them to hang down below the branches. This means that the branches must be well spaced so that there is plenty of room for both flowers and fruit to be displayed without becoming entangled with the foliage on the next branch. Many commercial bonsai are sensibly planted on rocks, which not only creates a dramatic image, contrasting with the tiny flowers and fruit, but also ensures adequate space below the lowest branches for the autumn fruit to be displayed.

Where to keep firethorn
All firethorn prefer to be exposed to full sun. In winter, hardy firethorn can survive under a blanket of snow for several weeks, but for safety move to a garage or shed in very bad weather. Tropical firethorn bonsai prefer full sun and are best kept outdoors in summer to maximize pollination. Keep above 7°C (45°F) in winter.

Maintenance
Repotting Repot young plants annually; older plants every two years. Use standard soil mix.

Pruning Prune to shape and remove unwanted branches straight after flowering; do not prune away too many flowering spurs which would spoil the display of fruit. Allow the new shoots that grow after pruning to extend untouched until the fruit has set and then cut back to three or four leaves. This shortened shoot will form the base of next year's flowering shoots.

Pinching Pinch the overextending shoots only during flowering and when fruit is ripe.

Watering Although tolerant of a little dryness around the roots from time to time, the tree will eventually start to die back if this is allowed to happen too often. Keep the soil evenly moist throughout the year, even in winter.

Feeding Balanced feed until flowering commences, then cease feeding. Resume when flowering has finished with low-nitrogen fertilizer. If the fruit falls before it has set, try using nitrogen-free feed after flowering next year. If reluctant to flower, apply low-nitrogen fertilizer throughout the growing season and change to nitrogen-free in autumn.

Beware! The shoots become brittle in their second year. Wire train new shoots while they are still green and pliable. The thorns are extremely sharp. If you snip off the tip of each thorn, you will not only make working on the tree a less painful experience, but you will also encourage the dormant buds at the sides of the thorn to develop.

The spectacular display of early-summer flowers is followed by masses of brilliant orange or red berries, which can remain on the tree right through the winter months.

Rhododendron indicum
Satsuki Azalea

Outdoor

In their native Japan, azalea bonsai are in a class of their own. Not only do the smooth orange-brown bark and small glossy leaves produce wonderful bonsai in their own right, but the profusion of flowers in late spring and early summer come in an almost infinite array of colours. Some varieties have self-coloured flowers and some bear flowers of two different colours on the same tree. Others even have pink-and-white variegated flowers. The flowers are borne at the tips of the previous year's shoots and, unlike normal garden azaleas, appear after vegetative growth has arisen from the buds immediately behind the flower bud.

Always buy azalea bonsai when they are in flower because it is impossible to describe the amazing flower colours on a simple label.

Where to keep satsuki azalea

Satsuki azaleas will tolerate full sun for a while but will perform at their best if kept in semi-shade, or even full shade during mid-summer. The flowers also last a lot longer in semi-shade. In winter, protect from wind at all times and bring the tree into a frost-free garage or shed if temperatures threaten to stay below -5°C (23°F) for more than a day or so.

Maintenance

Repotting Repot young plants every two years; old plants every four or five years, immediately after flowering. Use only lime-free ingredients, preferably opting for a proprietary ericaceous compost or sphagnum peat for the organic content. Use the standard soil mix with an extra 20 per cent organic matter. Add a few handfuls of chopped fresh sphagnum moss to keep the soil aerated and to enhance both drainage and water retention.

The variety of colour in the flowers of satsuki azaleas is almost infinite. But even without flowers, the sinuous orange-brown trunk and neat glossy foliage make the species ideal for bonsai of all sizes.

Pruning Prune branches and cut back all excess growth immediately after flowering. Do not prune until the same time the following year unless you want to remodel the bonsai.

Pinching Pinch out the tips of overextending shoots to keep the tree in trim. Do not pinch out all growing tips in summer or you will find you have thrown away all next year's flowers.

Watering Azaleas will not tolerate drought, so the soil must not be allowed to become even partially dry. Keep the soil moist but not too wet throughout the year. Azaleas are lime-haters and will rapidly deteriorate if calcium is allowed to build up in the soil. Use rainwater or lime-free tap water. If you cannot use either, treat the soil with a proprietary soil acidifier.

Feeding Weak solution of balanced feed until flowering commences, then cease feeding. Resume only when flowering has finished with low-nitrogen fertilizer until the end of autumn. Ensure that any fertilizers used are suitable for ericaceous plants, or use organic fertilizers.

Beware! The shoots and branches are very brittle and can snap without warning when being wire trained.

Sageretia theezans
Sageretia

Indoor & Outdoor

Originally from China, sageretia is used for commercial bonsai production throughout the Far East. It is one of the most popular species of indoor bonsai, ideal for the first-timer. The bark is a smooth grey-buff but flakes away in irregular patches to reveal lighter shades beneath, rewarding you with an ever-changing pattern. Branches that are a few years old and exposed roots also adopt this characteristic.

When young, the shoots are surprisingly brittle, but they become more supple in time, so any wiring should be done after they have begun to mature. However, although the shoots emerge from the parent branch at a wide angle, sometimes as much as 90 degrees, very little wiring should be necessary.

Tiny leaves, vigorous growth and colourful, flaky bark make sageretia an ideal species for the novice.

Where to keep sageretia

If close to a sunny window, provide shade in the form of an open-weave net curtain. Sageretias appreciate fresh air, so, if possible, keep outdoors in summer, in dappled shade. Bring indoors at night in early and late summer, when nights can be chilly. In winter, temperatures must be maintained above 12°C (54°F). When kept above 17°C (63°F), the tree may continue growing all winter if placed in a bright situation.

Maintenance

Repotting Every two to three years. Use a very sharp tool to cut the tough thicker roots. Use the standard soil mix or Akadama.

Pruning The wood is very hard and requires sharp tools and a strong grip. Pruning can take place at any time of year but is best done in mid-winter. Thin out crowded areas when growth has stopped or is at its slowest. But if

you want to build up the foliage mass on an underdeveloped branch, prune the branch back in mid-summer for vigorous new growth.

Pinching Shoots are too tough and too numerous to pinch with the fingers effectively. Use sharp scissors to trim the foliage to shape, but don't cut through individual leaves or they will discolour and spoil the tree.

Watering Sageretias are not thirsty and can tolerate dry roots. Water prolifically during the summer and whenever the tree is growing. Ease off the water a little as growth slows or stops in winter. Never spray the foliage.

Feeding Balanced feed while actively growing. Reduce frequency as growth slows down and cease if growth stops. Wait for two weeks after growth recommences before resuming feeding.

Beware! The two worst enemies of sageretia are cold draughts and dry air. Keep local humidity high by standing the pot over a tray of water and protect from draughts at all times. Mildew is a major problem, as is white fly.

Serissa foetida
Tree of a Thousand Stars

Indoor

This plant is a charming subject for bonsai, with tiny glossy leaves, bark that quickly becomes fissured and gnarled, and a willingness to produce masses of minute, white, trumpet-shaped flowers at any time of year. Although little more than a low, spreading shrub in the wild, with careful training it will develop strong, vertical trunks. Multi-trunked styles or group plantings are produced to maximize the foliage and flowers with relatively immature material.

Because serissas are such vigorous growers, they are one of the most popular species and are ideal for the beginner. It is worth buying several small trees and planting them in larger pots to encourage them to gain bulk rapidly while you practise your techniques on them.

Where to keep serissa

Serissas are able to bounce back after various traumas like cold draughts, a short period of dry soil and so on, but to be safe don't expose your serissa to temperatures below 12°C (54°F). Ideally, keep the temperature above 20°C (68°F) all year round. Serissas will take full sun provided the heat does not cause the soil to dry out. Using a deep pot can help.

Maintenance

Repotting Every two to three years in early spring. It is not for nothing that this species is called *foetida*, as the roots and lower trunk emit an obnoxious smell when wet – which they always are. Use the standard soil mix with an extra 20 per cent organic matter.

Pruning Prune unwanted branches at any time. Thin out overcrowded areas when growth is at its slowest to avoid inducing excessive adventitious shoots. Pruning in summer will cause masses of vigorous shoots to appear at many points in the vicinity of the cut.

Pinching Use nail scissors to trim the foliage clouds to shape. Avoid cutting through leaves, as this will cause them to discolour.

Watering Serissas love a really humid atmosphere. Do not overwater or stand for hours in water. Spray often with tepid water.

Feeding Balanced feed while the tree is actively growing. If growth continues in winter, apply weak low-nitrogen fertilizer.

Beware! Although serissas like moisture in the soil and a humid atmosphere, the flowers do not last as well if they remain damp for too long. Do not wet the flowers when watering and ensure that there is good air circulation when spraying so that the flowers dry quickly.

The tree of a thousand stars is normally trained with a bizarrely shaped trunk, accentuated by the stringy bark. The minute leaves and profusion of white flowers make this species one of the most popular of all indoor bonsai.

Stewartia monadelpha
Stewartia/Stuartia

Outdoor

This dwarf variety of the native Japanese species is one of the few bonsai subjects that looks better in winter and early spring than at any other time. The smooth, orange bark, which even covers the current year's growth, glows like fire against the dark sky, and the upward-pointing buds look like green candle flames.

Stewartias have a strong vertical habit which makes broad, spreading styles impractical.

Where to keep stewartia

Stewartias can tolerate hot sun but prefer slightly dappled shade, especially in really hot weather. Drying winds can also cause leaf margins to scorch. The ideal position is where the tree receives full sun in the morning but is shaded from mid-day onwards by a nearby tree or house so that there is still good overhead light. In winter, stewartias will withstand several degrees of frost for short periods, but should be placed in a frost-free shed or garage in really cold weather. Try not to expose to temperatures below -5°C (23°F).

Maintenance

Repotting Every two to five years in early spring, cutting thick roots back hard. Use only guaranteed lime-free soil ingredients such as ericaceous composts or sphagnum peat. A mix of 80 per cent organic matter and 20 per cent grit will help retain sufficient moisture.

Pruning Prune branches in early spring, three weeks before repotting. Hollow out the wounds and seal them to prevent unsightly swelling as they heal. Prune back the previous season's shoots to an outward-facing bud.

Pinching Pinch out the growing tip of all shoots as soon as two full leaves have been produced. Continue throughout the growing season. Remove any unwanted adventitious or inward-growing shoots as soon as they appear.

Watering Stewartias are water-lovers as well as lime-haters, so if you want to keep one and your tap water is hard (lime-rich), you will need to collect an awful lot of rainwater! Keep the soil as wet as possible without becoming waterlogged all year, slightly less so in winter.

Feeding Balanced feed during summer and nitrogen-free in autumn. Use only ericaceous fertilizers or those specially for lime-haters.

Beware! It will probably take you a couple of seasons to get the maintenance of challenging stewartia right, but you will be well rewarded.

Although the flowers and foliage of stewartia are both attractive in their own right, most bonsai connoisseurs prefer the winter image, when the striking orange bark and flame-shaped buds can be fully appreciated.

Ulmus parvifolia
Chinese Elm

Indoor & Outdoor

This is the perfect species for the newcomer to bonsai. It can be grown indoors or out, can withstand sun and cold, has small leaves and produces new shoots freely from all parts of the tree. The leaves are borne alternately at regular, short intervals on the shoots and, after pinching, a new shoot appears from the base of almost every leaf. This produces a herringbone pattern of growth which is so predictable that even the novice can quickly learn to prune and shape with complete confidence.

There are several forms of Chinese elm, some with smooth bark and others that rapidly develop thick, corky bark. The smooth-bark varieties tend to be slightly less hardy and need acclimatizing before being exposed to the cold.

Where to keep Chinese elm

Full sun is fine in early and late summer, but some light shade is beneficial in the hottest months. Dappled shade is mandatory if Chinese elms are kept indoors, close to a sunny window, but they are perfectly happy in shadier conditions. In fact, the leaf condition and autumn colour might even improve, although growth will be coarser. In winter, Chinese elms are deciduous if kept outdoors and more or less evergreen indoors. Temperatures below -5°C (23°F) can cause root damage and die-back of fine shoots. Shelter from winds and prolonged rain. Chinese elms may suffer foliage loss after a change in position or local environment, but will soon recover.

Maintenance

Repotting Every one to three years in early spring. The bark on the roots is slimy and fibrous and is easily damaged if blunt tools are used. Use the standard soil mix or Akadama.

Chinese elms rapidly produce a fine, dense tracery of twigs, bearing small, neat leaves. The bark of some varieties also becomes deeply fissured at a fairly young age.

Pruning Prune unwanted branches in early spring, three weeks before or after repotting. Pruning in mid-summer will generate masses of new growth around the wound. Strengthen weak branches by hard pruning in mid-summer and allowing the new shoots to bolt.

Pinching Pinch out the tops of all new shoots, leaving one or two leaves on each. Thin out congested areas and dead shoots as it becomes necessary, probably at least twice a year.

Watering Keep evenly moist in summer and only slightly drier in winter. Chinese elms can be especially thirsty in spring and early summer.

Feeding Balanced feed while the tree is actively growing. If growth continues in winter, apply weak low-nitrogen fertilizer. Outdoors, apply nitrogen-free feed in autumn.

Beware! Never use systemic insecticides or fungicides, which can cause total defoliation and considerable loss of vigour, resulting in die-back. This species is relatively pest-free.

Wisteria
Wisteria

Outdoor

Wisterias are probably the most spectacular of all garden climbers, with their profusion of purple to pink hanging racemes of small pea-like flowers that appear in late spring and early summer. They are also one of the most spectacular bonsai species – when in flower.

A wisteria bonsai consists of little more than an interesting trunk and sparse, stubby branches which form the framework for the year's frantic activity. Branches can normally be developed and improved by selective pruning alone and wiring only becomes necessary in the early stages of development. In time, the trunk and branches will become every bit as characterful as ancient full-sized plants.

Wisteria can make interesting trees even without flowers, but it is the June display of cascading lilac blooms that are the real appeal of this species.

Where to keep wisteria

Wisterias are designed to have their roots in the cool, moist, humus-rich soil in the shade of taller trees, with their shoots climbing through the canopy until their leaves are exposed to full sun. Imitate these conditions in the garden, shading the pot and spraying it liberally with water to keep it cool and moist. In winter, the roots can suffer damage in prolonged freezing conditions, especially when wet, so protect against the worst weather. Wisterias can do quite well if kept in a well-ventilated conservatory or cool greenhouse all year, provided temperatures fall regularly to below 10°C (50°F).

Maintenance

Repotting Every three years or so in early spring. Check annually to see if the roots have become pot-bound. If so, repot immediately; if not, wait another year. Select a deep pot to keep roots cool and moist and to balance visually the pendulous flowers. Use the standard soil mix with extra organic matter, or Akadama.

Pruning Structural pruning such as branch removal or shortening the trunk can be done in early spring. The routine pruning technique used on wisteria is designed to encourage flowers. Cut hard back straight after flowering, removing about half the flower-bearing stubs. Allow all subsequent growth total freedom until the rapidly extending shoots begin to become a nuisance and then cut back to two or three buds. Repeat several times each year.

Pinching Don't pinch.

Watering Water as lavishly as you like during summer. Deep pots can even be stood in water without the risk of 'drowning' the tree.

Feeding Low-nitrogen feed liberally applied from the end of flowering until early autumn, then switch to nitrogen-free feed.

Beware! Hot, dry roots quickly shrivel and die, sometimes killing one side of the tree.

Zelkova serrata
Zelkova/Grey Bark Elm

Outdoor

The natural habit of zelkovas is that of the archetypal tree – a straight, cylindrical trunk that is clear of branches for about 2 m (6½ ft), at which point it divides into branches that fan out and fork uniformly in all directions. Zelkova bonsai follow the same pattern in miniature and are created by shortening the trunk of a young sapling in mid-summer and training the shoots that emerge from the wound into branches. Very little wiring is necessary because the growth is uniform and generally well distributed, allowing the fan-like branch structure to be developed by pruning.

The bark remains smooth and relatively featureless throughout the tree's life, but this is in harmony with the elegant, gentle tapering of the branches into the tracery of fine twigs.

Some nurseries offer a plant called *Zelkova sinica*, but these are generally a variety of Chinese elm *(Ulmus parviflora)* that has been renamed, probably to avoid import restrictions.

Where to keep zelkova

Zelkovas are happy in full sun, although in really hot weather the leaves may scorch or turn yellow. Move to semi-shade in high summer, returning it to the sun in late summer or early autumn to enhance autumn coloration. If kept in semi-shade all year, the leaves will retain their spring colour – a bronze tint often edged with deep red – well into summer. In winter, the roots will withstand freezing, but the delicate fine twigs may die back. Winter protection from the wind is mandatory.

In the wild, zelkovas naturally form large, dome-shaped trees. This habit is echoed in bonsai, and a convincing little tree like this can be achieved in just a few years.

Maintenance

Repotting Every one to three years, depending on size and age, in early spring. Pay attention to the formation of the root buttress at the base of the trunk and prune away crossing or unsightly roots. Use the standard soil mix or Akadama.

Pruning Prune unwanted branches in early spring, two weeks before repotting. Strengthen weak branches by pruning them hard in mid-summer and allowing the resulting new shoots free rein until autumn.

Pinching Pinch out the tops of all new shoots as soon as two leaves have formed.

Watering Keep the soil evenly moist all year. Spray foliage at each watering to keep fresh; spray the trunk to keep it free of algae.

Feeding Balanced feed from spring to late summer, then change to nitrogen-free until the leaves have turned colour.

Beware! Zelkovas can become congested, especially at the top, which can result in die-back of many fine twigs. Regular thinning of crowded areas is essential.

Appendix

How can you take a
summer holiday when
your bonsai need daily
watering at that time of
year? How on earth can
they survive sub-zero
temperatures in winter?
What tools will you need
to buy? Here are some
answers...

While you are away

Providing the daily attention a bonsai requires is easy enough for most of the year, but you will inevitably want to take a holiday at some point. True bonsai devotees will either not take holidays at all or will arrange them during the winter months, when their trees demand less frequent attention and can generally be left unattended for a couple of weeks. But most of us prefer to take our holidays in the summer. So what measures can we take to ensure that our precious trees are still alive and healthy when we return?

Care services

Most reputable specialist bonsai nurseries will offer a holiday care service for a small fee – or even free – provided your collection isn't too extensive. In this case, you have the reassurance of knowing that your bonsai are being cared for by people who have the knowledge and skill to do the job properly, and who may well be able to notice any problems that you might have overlooked, such as difficult-to-spot pests or certain diseases.

It only takes a few minutes to erect a makeshift winter shelter utilizing some old building blocks and a sheet of clear polythene.

Good neighbours

Friends and neighbours are usually willing to water your trees for you for short periods. In fact, many would be quite honoured to be asked. But remember that, unless they too are bonsai enthusiasts, they will need a thorough training. Invite them round to watch you carry out routine watering. Explain the importance of a thorough watering and point out which trees require more than others. Overwatering is not likely to be a problem for two weeks in summer, whereas drought certainly will!

Capillary watering

If you can't find someone to help you out, try capillary matting, used in greenhouses and available from most garden nurseries. Cut a piece to fit snugly inside the base of the pot and some long strips that are passed up through the drainage holes. (Take care when easing the tree from the pot and replacing it after positioning the matting.) Stand the pot on stones to raise the strips of matting clear of the bench and immerse the free ends of the strips in a reservoir of water. The strips act as wicks and draw water through the drainage holes and saturate the matting inside the pot. Although this does not ensure even distribution of water throughout the pot, it will keep the tree alive for as long as the reservoir lasts. Place both tree and reservoir in the shade.

Last resort

If all else fails, find the shadiest corner of the garden and bury the pots in the ground, ensuring that the surface of the soil in the pots is below ground level. Scatter some slug pellets around the area, but not too close to the trunks. Finally, water the surrounding area well and erect a temporary polythene tent over the trees to conserve as much water as possible. In theory, this method should keep the trees well for several weeks, the only danger being if the sun is allowed to fall on the polythene tent and causes the surface of the ground to dry out.

Outdoor bonsai in winter

Although most temperate species that are used for bonsai are hardy, that is able to withstand freezing, when grown in containers they don't have the advantage of their roots being buried deep in the ground where they are insulated to a certain extent from the cold. They also have fewer buds and finer twigs and shoots, which the cold can penetrate more easily.

Most hardy species will tolerate frozen roots for a short time, some for quite long periods, provided that no demand is placed on them. If the daytime temperature increases so that the buds begin to swell, or the wind causes dehydration of fine shoots or evergreen needles, frozen roots will not be able to replace the lost moisture. Having said that, many hardy species, particularly conifers, actually need a period of sub-zero temperatures in order to remain healthy and build up vigour for the spring growth surge.

The secret of success is to allow the trees to undergo the natural dormancy process, but to protect them from the most dangerous of the elements: wind and excessive rain.

If you can provide a polytunnel (polythene greenhouse) for your trees during winter, your problems will largely be solved. This will allow light and air to reach the trees, but will shelter them from both wind and rain. If this is not possible, you can cover the display benches with clear polythene and place the trees underneath, standing the pots on bricks to keep them off the ground.

Whether your trees are in a polytunnel or in makeshift winter quarters, you will need to check them each week to make sure that the pots are not drying out. In mild weather, open the tunnel or tent for a few hours to allow a change of air.

If neither of these provisions is possible, there is still one course of action you can take.

Many hardy deciduous species will take overnight frost without any trouble, and provide you with a beautifully emphasized tracery of fine shoots.

Conifers can be placed against a fence or wall where they are sheltered from the wind. Cover the surface of the pots with plastic bags to keep off the worst of the rain. Large deciduous bonsai (except trident maples and Chinese elms) can receive similar treatment.

Smaller trees, and Chinese elms and trident maples of all sizes, should be eased from their pots and planted in the ground in a sheltered corner of the garden. Ensure the top of the root ball is at least 2.5 cm (1 in) or so beneath ground level. It is a good idea to buy some horticultural fleece (a fibrous sheeting – extremely lightweight and with excellent insulating properties) to drape over the tops of the trees. This will allow passage of rain, but greatly reduces the wind and maintains a temperature beneath which is constantly several degrees higher than outside.

The only danger with the latter type of winter provision is that soil-borne pests may attack the roots. This will not normally happen in the depth of winter, but as spring approaches and the soil warms up, pests become active. You would be wise not to leave it too late before lifting your trees from the ground and replacing them in their pots.

Tools

To begin with, rather than buying specialist tools, you can do just as well with normal household or garden tools. You will need secateurs, small scissors, pliers and wire cutters – make sure they are all sharp. As you become more involved in your hobby, you will begin to build up your own collection of specialist tools. This selection will give you an idea of the most common bonsai tools and their uses.

Angled side cutters for pruning branches

Strong shears for pruning roots

Fine-pointed scissors for pruning shoots

Coconut-fibre brush for tidying the soil

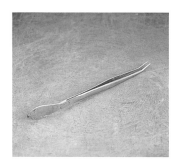

Tweezers to make tip pinching easier

Wire cutters that cut right to the tip

Small root rake, for weeding pots

Glossary

This glossary includes botanical and arboricultural terms that are relevant to bonsai culture as well as terms that are unique to bonsai.

Acid Soils with a pH content of less than 7.0. Although most trees will grow happily in acid soil, some, including field maple (*Acer campestre*) and beech (*Fagus sylvatica*), do better in more alkaline conditions. Others, particularly azaleas, rhododendrons and some heathers, thrive only in acid soils.

Acuminate Tapering to a fine point, usually in leaf shapes.

Alkaline A term describing soils with a pH content of more than 7.0, or calcium rich. Although many trees will grow happily in alkaline soil, others prefer more acid conditions. Some species, including azaleas, rhododendrons, and some heathers, will not tolerate alkaline soil at all. These plants are known as calcifuges.

Alternate Describing leaves or buds that are placed singly at different levels on alternate sides of a shoot.

Apex The tip of a shoot or root, or of a tree, from which extension growth takes place. In bonsai, this point is decided upon for aesthetic reasons and is not necessarily the focus of the plant's energy.

Axil, axillary The angle between a leaf and the stem from which future growth can emerge. The angle between the midrib and the vein of a leaf.

Bankan Bonsai style: a tree with a twisted or coiled trunk.

Basal Applied to fresh growth arising from the base of a plant.

Bonkei A 'potted landscape' consisting of rocks, small trees and other plants, always with miniature figures, houses or bridges.

Bonsai Literally a 'potted plant', the term has now come to mean the (traditionally Chinese and Japanese) art of creating in miniature the splendour of a fully grown tree by meticulous pruning and shaping of a tree growing in a (usually shallow) container.

Break To grow out from an axillary bud. This growth pattern is often natural, but in bonsai it is the result of pruning or pinching current shoots, and forms the basis of most refinement techniques as well as the Lignan or grow-and-clip method of development.

Broad-leaved Denotes any tree other than conifers.

Broom Bonsai style: generally based on the natural growth habit of zelkova, where all the branches arise from the same point, at the top of a straight trunk. All branches are more or less equal in weight and subdivide at diminishing intervals, forming a dome-shaped crown. Japanese term: Hokidachi.

Bud notching Cutting a small crescent of bark from above a bud to stimulate growth from that bud and to encourage a wide angle between the resulting shoot and the main branch.

Bunjingi Bonsai style: the only named style to originate in China and based on the representations of trees in the paintings of the southern school of landscape painting which began back in the Tang dynasty (618–907). The name derives from the scholars known as *Wen-jen* or 'men of books'.

Buttress Exaggerated thickening of the trunk base at the point where the surface roots emerge. This feature gives a tree a feeling of stability and strength.

Calcifuge Plant that cannot tolerate the presence of lime in the soil or a pH of more than 7.0. Rhododendrons, azaleas and heathers are among these.

Channelled Describing a leaf whose margins curl upwards, forming a channel.

Chokkan Bonsai style: a tree with a straight upright trunk known as 'formal upright'. The ideal chokkan bonsai will have a perfectly straight trunk with uniform taper and branch structure and an overall conical shape. The roots should be spread evenly around the base.

Classification The internationally recognized system of classifying plants by their Latin names.

Clone Identical plants arising from a single parent and reproduced vegetatively.

Columnar Describes a tree that is tall and narrow with straight, more or less parallel sides.

Conifer A cone-bearing tree, with needle-like or linear leaves.

Container-grown Young nursery stock that has been raised in pots.

Coppicing The practice of cutting trees back to their base in order to encourage the growth of several new stems, invariably carried out on deciduous species.

Cutting A section of stem leaf or root that is taken in order to propagate the plant and maintain identical characteristics.

Damping off A disease that attacks young seedlings which may be caused by several different fungi, resulting in the stems collapsing at ground level and killing the plant. It is encouraged by cold wet soils, overcrowding or poor air circulation around the stem. Damping off may be prevented by watering the compost with Cheshunt compound when sowing, and again once the seedlings have germinated. Other precautions include avoiding reusing old composts and thoroughly cleaning all seed trays and tools before use to ensure that no trace of the disease remains.

Deciduous Describes a tree or shrub that loses its leaves at the end of each growing season.

Deltoid Describes a leaf that is triangular shaped or with curved basal angles; for example, the leaf of the silver birch.

Derris An insecticide obtained from the root of a tropical climbing plant. Although it is not as effective as modern synthetic insecticides, it is kinder to the plant and less persistent.

Die-back When shoots, twigs and sometimes whole branches wither and dry out. Major causes include drought (birches, willow), late spring frosts (Japanese maples, Chinese elm, etc.) and severe winter weather (most imported plants). Root damage or disease can also cause die-back.

Disbudding Removing unwanted buds in order to direct the plant's energy into the remaining ones. This may be done to increase the size and quality of blooms, but in bonsai it is more often used as a shaping technique, especially with shohin (small-size) bonsai.

Division Propagation by separating sections from the root mass of a plant. These sections must have buds or shoots as well as adequate roots. Most trees and shrubs that either naturally grow in clumps, such as hazel, or that sucker profusely, such as elm, can be propagated this way.

Drainage Probably the most important factor in bonsai composts, drainage is the free passage of water downwards through the compost and its dispersal through the drainage holes in the base of the pot. Poor drainage will give rise to waterlogged soil, which in turn will provide ideal conditions for root-rotting fungi. It will also prevent sufficient air space, thus further weakening the roots.

Driftwood Bonsai style: sharimiki, comprising large areas of bare, bleached wood, often carved into detailed abstract designs. This style above all others creates the impression of age and durability.

Dwarf A genetic mutation of a species, producing a much lower, slower and more compact growth pattern. Some dwarf species make good bonsai, and their use should only be considered cheating if their natural habit is relied upon too heavily at the expense of more precise bonsai training techniques.

Fastigiate Describes a tall, narrow, columnar growth habit, usually of trees and shrubs, where all the branches sweep sharply upwards.

Feathering A process by which the lower branches of young saplings are retained for a few years in order to thicken and strengthen the trunk.

Fire-blight A severe and almost inevitably fatal fungal disease of trees, particularly those of the family Rosaceae (cherries, apples, cotoneaster, pyracantha, etc.).

Forcing Accelerating the growth cycle of a plant by artificially changing its growing conditions. The most common application of this technique in bonsai is to encourage late spring-flowering trees to produce flowers early in time for exhibitions.

Fukinagashi Bonsai style: windswept. Although this is one of the most dramatic of all bonsai styles, it is one of the most difficult to achieve convincingly.

Genus A group of closely related species. For example, all the cherries, apricots and plums belong to the genus *Prunus*. The plural is genera.

Go-kan Bonsai style: with five trunks. The individual trunks may be upright, slanted or curved.

Grafting The bonding of one part of a woody plant to another, usually on a separate plant.

Han-kengai Bonsai style: semi-cascade. This, as the name implies, is one of those 'in between' styles whose exact definition is elusive. The most commonly accepted definition is a tree whose leader or most dominant low branch (which must be greater than the ascending leader) cascades below the rim of the pot but not below the base.

Half-hardy *see* **Hardy**.

Hardening-off The process of gradually introducing a plant that has been grown in sheltered or protected conditions to the rigours of the outside environment. This is done by allowing it to stay outside in the open during the day, or in mild spells, and returning the plant to its protection at night.

Hardy Describes a plant that is able to survive outside in winter.

Hokidachi Bonsai style: known as broom or besom. This is probably the most 'tree-like' of all bonsai styles and consists of a number of branches all issuing from the same point at the top of an upright trunk. These branches divide and subdivide regularly until they form a fine tracery of twigs.

Hybrid The offspring of parents of different species, or different forms of a species.

Ikadabuki Bonsai style: raft. This style is created by laying a tree on its side and training all the conveniently placed branches upwards. All the branches that point downwards or that are not suitably sited are removed. The original trunk is then buried in the soil and eventually produces roots along its length. The new trunks are then trained in the normal way into any suitable style. This is an ideal method for producing group plantings since there is no competition between plants.

Inflorescence The flower-bearing part of a plant.

Internode The distance between the leaf nodes on a shoot. It is this that dictates whether or not a plant has the growth characteristics suitable for bonsai culture.

Jin The most commonly used Japanese term in bonsai culture and one of the most difficult to define concisely. A jin is a branch or the apex of a tree that has had its bark removed and has been treated with a preservation bleach such as lime sulphur in order to simulate the naturally occurring dead, sun-bleached branches commonly found on old pines and junipers. The appearance of great age and a lifetime's struggle against the elements can be bestowed on a bonsai by the use of jins, which may also be carved and shaped into abstract sculptural forms.

Jukei The Japanese word for 'style', describing the shape or form of a bonsai.

Kabudachi Bonsai style: clump style, where all the trunks emanate from closely located points on the same root. This style is often created by cutting a trunk down to ground level and allowing several new trunks to grow from around the cut. In full-sized trees, this process is known as coppicing.

Kengai Bonsai style: cascade. To qualify as a true cascade, the lowest point of the tree must be below the bottom of its container.

Korabuki Bonsai style: multi-trunked planting.

Kyonal A proprietary Japanese product used for dressing wounds after pruning. It has a plasticine-like consistency, but never dries out or goes hard. This means that,

as the wound heals, the Kyonal is forced out and does not become enveloped by the new growth. It is easy to use and coloured so as to conceal the wound and blend with the bark.

Kyuhon-yose Bonsai style: nine-trunked planting.

Layering A means of propagation from woody shoots or branches involving the removal of a band of bark around the chosen shoot about one-and-a-half times the thickness of the shoot. The shoot is then either pegged to the ground and covered with soil or wrapped with damp sphagnum moss and enclosed in polythene. Once roots appear and have established, the shoot can be severed from the parent and potted up.

Leaching The process by which nutrients and other soluble minerals are removed from the soil by water draining through. To counteract this, bonsai growers recommend applying more regular but weaker feeds.

Leader The main, vertical stem or shoot of a young plant. The dominant shoot that extends fastest and dictates the directional thrust of the tree's growth. Also used to describe the dominant shoot on a branch or smaller twig.

Leaf mould Partially decayed dead leaves that have broken down to a crumbly texture. Deciduous leaves, especially oak and beech, are suitable for deciduous trees; pine needle mould is best for pines. A mixture of the two used instead of peat will benefit the trees and is less environmentally destructive.

Loam A soil that is neither heavy and sticky nor dry and sandy. Good loam contains clay, sand, humus and silt, and is both moisture retentive and free-draining.

Maiden A newly grafted tree, usually only a year or so old, still

in the early stages of training. Normally applied to fruit trees.

Mame bonsai Miniature bonsai. Sources vary in the actual definition of the size of mame: some books of Japanese origin state 10 cm (4 in) high, others 15 cm (6 in) high. The general consensus seems to be that a mame bonsai is one that can easily be held on the flat palm of a hand.

Matsu Japanese for pine.

Moyogi Bonsai style: informal upright. This is the most commonly grown style and has come to encompass many of those trees that do not fall comfortably into another style. The traditional moyogi has a trunk that gently bends first one way, then the other in ever-diminishing curves, throwing out a branch on each outer curve convexity.

Native A plant that is believed to have arrived in this country without the influence of mankind.

Neagari Bonsai style: exposed root. Ironically, this style is more commonly found in penjing – the original Chinese form of bonsai – than it is in Japanese trees.

Nebari The visible surface roots of a bonsai. Ideally, these should radiate evenly but not uniformly all around the base of the trunk. They should emerge gradually from the trunk and should enter the soil in a natural manner.

Netsuranari Bonsai style: root-connected style – several trees that all grow from the same root. The trees themselves may be individually trained in any style that suits the species and multi-trunk planting. Naturally occurring netsuranari are root suckers – as in elm or some species of *Prunus*.

Nitrogen One of the three major chemical elements necessary for plant growth. Nitrogen is responsible for healthy leaf and shoot growth, but too much may result in over-vigorous, sappy growth. Nitrogen deficiency results in weak growth and small, yellowish leaves.

pH The pH scale is a means of quantifying the acid/alkaline balance of a soil or compost. The neutral point that suits most plants is around 7.0. A lower figure indicates increased acidity and a higher figure indicates increased alkalinity. Although some plants prefer acid conditions and others prefer alkaline, their range is limited to 4.5–9. The addition of lime to the soil can increase its pH balance or it can be decreased by using proprietary products.

Phosphates One of the three major plant nutrients, phosphates are responsible for healthy and vigorous roots and also assist in protecting against diseases.

Pinching Removing the growing tips of the shoots while still soft using the fingernails or, in the case of most conifers, by gently rolling the tip between finger and thumb.

Pollarding The ancient practice of cutting back all branches to the trunk every few years in order to put the long growths, which regenerate after pollarding, to a variety of uses. Traditionally carried out on willow and ash, pollarded oaks, wych elms and hornbeams are also common.

Potash A potassium carbonate fertilizer used to balance the effects of nitrogen. Essential to flower production, it protects against disease and harsh conditions.

Propagation The increase of plants by either seed, cutting, layering, division, grafting or, nowadays, tissue culture.

Pruning The controlled cutting back of woody parts of a plant, either to promote new growth, to influence the flowering pattern or to aid in the shaping. It is possible to style bonsai using pruning as

the only shaping technique, as demonstrated by the Chinese Lignan school, also known as the clip-and-grow style.

Respiration The 'breathing' action of a plant. The process involves the exchange of oxygen from the atmosphere with carbon dioxide, which is released during the conversion of store foods into plant energy. In effect, the reverse of photosynthesis.

Sabamiki *see* **Sharimiki**.

Sankan Bonsai style: triple-trunk. The attitudes of the tree may be upright, slanting, windswept or any other suitable design.

Sapwood The living wood forming the outer layers of the trunk or thick branch of a tree. The sapwood consists of several annual rings and is the means through which water and water-borne nutrients are conducted up the tree. Once the sapwood has outlived its usefulness, it in effect dies and hardens to form the structural heartwood which gives the tree its strength.

Sekijoju Bonsai style: root-over-rock planting.

Shakan Bonsai style: slanting.

Sharimiki A portion of the trunk of a bonsai that has had the bark removed and the exposed wood textured and bleached to emulate weather-torn trees in exposed mountain sites.

Sokan Bonsai style: double or twin-trunk.

Spur A short lateral side growth that only produces a very short extension each year and usually bears the flower buds.

Sucker A shoot arising from the roots or the underground part of a trunk. Suckers often form a tree's major means of propagation, as with elms.

Tap root The main downward-growing root of a plant or young tree. These roots seldom go down more than 1.5–1.8 m (5–6 ft). Young seedlings and nursery stock will have tap roots that should be cut as high up as possible without removing too many side roots before training begins.

Tender Describes any plant that cannot tolerate frost and is liable to damage or death in freezing conditions. All trees sold as indoor bonsai should be treated as tender.

Terminal Refers to the upper shoot, flower or bud. This can be either on the leader (main upward-growing branch) or on a lateral or sideways-growing branch.

Truncate Describes a leaf whose base, adjacent to the petiole, is flat.

Variegated Applies to leaves that are patterned with patches of a contrasting colour, occasionally pink, more often shades of cream or yellow. The unpredictable nature of this patterning and its effect make variegated plants unsuitable for bonsai.

Variety A variation on the species, either naturally occurring or artificially induced.

Vegetative Propagation by a variety of means other than by seed, for example cuttings, layering, division or grafting.

Whorl An arrangement of leaves or needles radiating from the same point, as in the non-extension growth of larch and cedar.

Yamadori Japanese bonsai term for a collected tree.

Yose-ue Bonsai style: group or multi-trunk.

Index

Page numbers in *italics* refer to the illustrations.

Acknowledgements

The publishers would like to thank Peter Chan at Heron Bonsai and Charlotte Dalampira at Tokonoma Bonsai for all their help in providing bonsai trees for photography.

Special Photography: Peter Myers and Michael Gomez

Bridgeman Art Library, London/New York/Fitzwilliam Museum, University of Cambridge 13
Peter Chan/Herons 18, 19 top, 19 Bottom
Corbis UK Ltd/Bettman 14 top
The Art Archive/Victoria & Albert Museum 17
Garden Picture Library/David Askham 78 centre/Christopher Fairweather 82 centre/JS Sira 116 centre/Brigitte Thomas 34 centre
Octopus Publishing Group Limited/George Wright 34 bottom
Colin Lewis 8, 35, 120, 121
Harry Smith Collection 98 right